Hunger and Human Rights:

The Politics of Famine in North Korea

Stephan Haggard

and Marcus Noland

U.S. Committee for Human Rights in North Korea

ISBN 0-9771-1110-5

Library of Congress Control Number: 2005931434

Hunger and Human Rights: The Politics of Famine in North Korea

U.S. Committee for Human Rights in North Korea

1101 15th Street, NW

Suite 800

Washington, DC 20005 USA

Designed by Stewart Andrews, Noodlebox Design, LLC

Debra Liang-Fenton, *Executive Director*
U.S. Committee for Human Rights in North Korea
1101 15th Street, NW, Suite 800
Washington, DC 20005 USA
Tel: (202) 467-4765
Fax: (202) 293-6042
Web: WWW.HRNK.ORG

Hunger and Human Rights:
The Politics of Famine in North Korea

Stephan Haggard is Lawrence and Sallye Krause Professor at the Graduate School of International Relations and Pacific Studies at the University of California, San Diego, where he serves as Director of the Korea-Pacific Program. From 2000 to 2001, he was Interim Dean of the Graduate School of International Relations and Pacific Studies. From 1997 to 1999, he was the Director of the Institute on Global Conflict and Cooperation, the University of California's policy center for international affairs. In that capacity, he chaired the Northeast Asian Cooperation Dialogue, a track-two diplomatic exercise in Northeast Asia. His research and teaching interests center on the political economy of the Asia-Pacific and Latin America. He is the author of *Pathways from the Periphery the Political Economy of Growth in the Newly Industrializing Countries* (1990) and *The Political Economy of Democratic Transitions* with Robert Kaufman (1995). His writings on the Asian financial crisis include: *The Political Economy of the Asian Financial Crisis* (2000); co-editor, *Economic Crisis and Corporate Restructuring in Korea* (2003); and on foreign direct investment in high-technology industries in the Asia-Pacific: *From Silicon Valley to Singapore: Location and Competitive Advantage in the Disk Drive Industry* with David McKendrick and Richard Doner (2000).

Marcus Noland is a Senior Fellow at the Institute for International Economics. He was a Senior Economist at the Council of Economic Advisers in the Executive Office of the President of the United States, and has held research or teaching positions at the Johns Hopkins University, the University of Southern California, Tokyo University, Saitama University, the University of Ghana, the Korea Development Institute, and the East-West Center. He has received fellowships sponsored by the Japan Society for the Promotion of Science, the Council on Foreign Relations, the Council for the International Exchange of Scholars, and the Pohang Iron and Steel Corporation (POSCO). Dr. Noland is the author of *Korea After Kim Jong-Il* (2004); *Avoiding the Apocalypse: The Future of the Two Koreas* (2000), which was awarded the prestigious Ohira Masayoshi Memorial Prize; and *Pacific Basin Developing Countries: Prospects for the Future* (1990). He is coauthor of *Industrial Policy in an Era of Globalization* with Howard Pack (2003); *Global Economic Effects of the Asian Currency Devaluations* (1998), *Reconcilable Differences? United States-Japan Economic Conflict* with C. Fred Bergsten (1993), and *Japan in the World Economy* with Bela Balassa (1988); coeditor of *Pacific Dynamism and the International Economic System* (1993); and editor of *Economic Integration of the Korean Peninsula* (1998).

Acknowledgments

In writing this report, we benefited mightily from a large "invisible college" of policymakers, humanitarian workers, and academics with an interest in North Korea.

We would like to thank Jaehoon Ahn, Christine Chang, Nicholas Eberstadt, L. Gordon Flake, Lola Gostelow, Cormac O. Grada, David Hawk, Amanda Hayes, Christopher Hughes, Erica Kang, Yeri Kim, Young-Hoon Kim, Tae-jin Kwon, Suk Lee, Young-sun Lee, Andrei Lankov, Sue Lautze, Wonhyuk Lim, Mark Manyin, Hans Maretzki, Chun Sang Moon, Sang-wook Nam, Takeshi Nagasawa, Syungje Park, Daniel Pinkston, Ed Reed, Hazel Smith, and Jae-Jean Suh. Our interviews included staff from the South Korean Ministry of Unification, the Korea Institute for National Unification, the Korea Rural Economic Institute, the Korea Institute for International Economic Policy, the World Food Program, and three anonymous readers commissioned by the U.S. Committee for Human Rights in North Korea. We also benefited enormously from off-the-record conversations with a number of current staff at official and non-governmental relief agencies, who, for obvious reasons of political sensitivity, requested anonymity. The government of North Korea regrettably declined to allow us to visit the Democratic People's Republic of Korea as part of this research, replying to our request that "the DPRK's official position [is] to have no relation with 'Human Rights' entities."

Paul Karner and Yeon-kyeong Kim provided outstanding research assistance.

This report was made possible through support provided by the Office of Transition Initiatives, Bureau for Democracy, Conflict and Human Rights and Humanitarian Assistance, U.S. Agency for International Development, under the terms of the OTI-G-00-04-00009-00. The opinions expressed herein are those of the authors and do not necessarily reflect the views of the U.S. Agency for International Development.

Regarding photography

The photographs in this report are used with the permission of DailyNK, a leading online news outlet for Information about North Korea established by the South Korean NGO Network for North Korean Democracy and Human Rights (NKNet). DailyNK is working with Japanese NGOs such as Rescue the North Korean People (RENK) to obtain visual images of life inside North Korea, and share them with the international community. The Committee is grateful to DailyNK and RENK for their contributions to this project.

Table of Contents

Preface

Václav Havel
Prague, 1 August 2005

In recent years we have met with a wave of terrorist attacks, with mass migration, with a deterioration of the environment, and with instability in many other areas. Besides this we hold lively debates about, and attempt to help effectively, the poorest countries and those who cannot exercise their basic civic and human rights. We experience many deep disagreements. But nowhere do we come up against a state as closed as North Korea, whose citizens live in utter isolation, who can avail of no human rights and who, what is more, are the victims of a centrally run, i.e. state-supported, humanitarian catastrophe. For the second decade, that country is experiencing a chronic shortage of food; the famine at the end of the 1990s was the direct cause of the deaths of at least one million people. That famine, however, need not have been North Korea's fate, if its own citizens had not been denied the most basic human rights.

The attached study documents, for instance, the parallel growth in humanitarian aid as the government of the Democratic People's Republic of Korea stopped importing food and gradually reduced the purchase of grain to as low as one-tenth. So instead of the destitute population being fed and supplies of food being supplemented thanks to international aid, the communist regime has saved the dollars raised in order to shore up its power.

After over ten years of humanitarian missions on the territory of North Korea, these programs are far from fulfilling international standards. We have no guarantee that aid is reaching the truly needy, and the communist regime consistently spoils any attempts to control its distribution. International solidarity is therefore abused directly by government structures, with the privileged army to the forefront. Furthermore, efforts to monitor needs and distribution in a more detailed manner by the World Food Programme are made relative by the direct imports of South Korea and China. The brutal regime supplies them only to the most loyal. If anyone bears even a sign of suspicion that he has lost blind faith, the suspect is immediately deprived of basic foodstuffs and medical aid; he loses his job and even the chance to receive an education. It is not unusual to end up in a system of concentration camps not dissimilar to the Soviet Gulags.

We stand before a huge ethical dilemma: Is it possible—and, if so, to what extent—to help starving North Koreans, whose fates depend on us a great deal more than on their government, if at the same time we are forever deceived and systematically blackmailed? An army armed with weapons of mass destruction is, to be sure, a permanent threat to the whole region. Let us recall that in the 1930s, Stalin unleashed a government-organized famine in Ukraine, the aim of which was to destroy the *kulaks* and to reinforce totalitarian power. In connection with the North Korean tragedy, we have therefore to pose the question whether through giving humanitarian aid we are at the same time reinforcing perhaps the worst political regime on the planet, a regime which is prepared to reinforce its power in the most drastic of means.

Executive Summary

North Korea is well into its second decade of chronic food shortages. A famine in the 1990s killed as many as one million North Koreans or roughly five percent of the population. North Korean claims that the famine was due primarily to natural disasters and external shocks are misleading in important respects. The decline in food production and the deterioration of the public distribution system (PDS) were visible years before the floods of 1995. Moreover, the government was culpably slow to take the necessary steps to guarantee adequate food supplies. With plausible policy adjustments—such as maintaining food imports on commercial terms or aggressively seeking multilateral assistance—the government could have avoided the famine and the shortages that continue to plague the country. Instead, the regime blocked humanitarian aid to the hardest hit parts of the country during the peak of the famine and curtailed commercial imports of food once humanitarian assistance began.

Coping responses by households during the famine contributed to a bottom-up marketization of the economy, ratified by the economic policy changes introduced by the North Korean government in 2002. What began as a socialist famine arising out of failed agricultural policies and a misguided emphasis on food self-sufficiency has evolved into a chronic food emergency more akin to those observed in market and transition economies. Incomplete reforms have not solved the problem of declining food production and have given rise to a large food-insecure population among the urban non-elite.

The world community has responded to this tragedy with considerable generosity, committing more than $2 billion in food aid to the country over the past decade. The United States has contributed more than $600 million, equivalent to 2 million metric tons of grain. Yet at virtually every point, the North Korean government has placed roadblocks in the way of the donor community, and more than 10 years into this process, the relief effort remains woefully below international standards in terms of transparency and effectiveness. Up to half of aid deliveries do not reach their intended recipients.

Due to these programmatic problems, diplomatic conflicts, and competing needs elsewhere in the world, patience with North Korea has waned among some major donors. In recent years, aid through the World Food Programme (WFP), the principle channel for delivering multilateral assistance, has consistently fallen short of its targets. At the same time, North Korea has been able to partly, if not fully, compensate for these shortfalls through generous assistance from South Korea and China. The bilateral assistance from these countries is weakly monitored, if conditional at all, and thus undercuts the ability of the WFP and other donors to negotiate improvements in the transparency, and ultimately, effectiveness, of multilateral assistance.

These problems cannot be separated from the underlying political situation in the country; it is misguided to separate the humanitarian and human rights discourses. North Korea would have faced difficulties in the 1990s regardless of its regime type. But it is difficult to imagine a famine of this magnitude, or chronic food shortages of this duration, occurring in a regime that protected basic political and civil liberties.

Introduction

The notion of famine conjures up disturbing images of emaciated people and wasting, listless children. Confronted with the devastating impact of inadequate caloric intake on the human body, one's understandable impulse is to think of famine in terms of physical shortages of food supplies. Yet in the contemporary world, the sources of food insecurity increasingly can be traced not to natural causes but to human ones. Today there is no reason for anyone to starve as a result of weather conditions, food shortages, or even failures in distribution. Global food supplies are adequate. Information on weather patterns and crop conditions is now readily available, providing an effective early warning system of potential shortfalls and crises. Global markets for basic grains are well developed and highly integrated and the world community has developed a well-institutionalized system of humanitarian assistance.

A series of international covenants have made explicit the commitment to a world without hunger. The 1948 Universal Declaration of Human Rights enshrined the right to adequate food. The 1966 International Covenant on Economic, Social and Cultural Rights (ICESCR) elaborated this commitment as "the fundamental right of everyone to be free from hunger." At the 1996 World Food Summit, official delegations from 185 countries, including representatives from the governments of the United States and the Democratic People's Republic of Korea (the DPRK or North Korea), reaffirmed "the right of everyone to have access to safe and nutritious food, consistent with the right to adequate food and the fundamental right of everyone to be free of hunger."[1]

When initially articulated, these rights looked more like pious wishes than achievable objectives. But an effective set of global institutions is now capable of making these political commitments viable by soliciting food contributions and delivering emergency assistance to populations facing distress from natural disasters and economic dislocation. With effective institutions and adequate physical supplies, the occurrence of famine increasingly signals not the lack of food or capacity, but some fundamental political or governance failure. Natural conditions are no longer our primary adversaries: humans are.

The case of North Korea, where a chronic food emergency is well into its second decade, is an egregious example of this phenomenon. Although estimates vary widely, a famine in the mid-1990s killed as many as one million North Koreans, or roughly five percent of the population. Millions more were left to contend with broken lives and personal misery. Particularly worrisome are the long-term effects—including irreversible ones—on the human development of infants and children.

Conditions in North Korea today are less tenuous than during the worst of the famine, thanks in part to humanitarian assistance from the world community. Yet despite this assistance, millions of North Koreans remain chronically food insecure. When the food crisis began, access to food came through a public distribution system (PDS) controlled by the regime and entitlements were partly a function of political status. As the socialist economy crumbled and markets developed in response to the state's inability to fulfill its obligations under the old social compact, the character of the crisis changed. Current shortages bear closer resemblance to food emergencies in market and transition economies, where access to food is determined by one's capacity to command resources in the marketplace. This type of emergency is no less severe, but poses different challenges to outside donors.

---

[1] Rome Declaration on World Food Security, November 1996, available at www.fao.org/documents/show_cdr.asp?url_file=/docrep/003/w3613e/w3613e00.htm.

Japanese food aid sold in Namhung Market in Anju, South Pyongan Province. The blue WFP logo and Japanese flag are printed on the bag, which states that the food was "donated by the Government of Japan." The date of production, October 2004, is printed on the bottom of the bag. This is part of the humanitarian assistance sent as the result of the May 2004 discussions between Japanese Prime Minister Junichiro Koizumi and North Korean leader Kim Jong Il. 125,000 tons were sent.

The world community has responded to this tragedy with considerable generosity, committing more than $2 billion in food aid to the country over the past decade. Despite its strained political relations with North Korea, the United States has been the largest donor of humanitarian assistance since 1995, contributing over $600 million in food aid, equivalent to over 2 million metric tons of grain. Yet a host of tensions and competing demands have contributed to fatigue among donors, including both the United States and Japan. These include diplomatic conflicts over the North Korean nuclear program and Japan's abductees; the apparent lack of progress in addressing the country's underlying economic problems; concerns about the transparency and effectiveness of the humanitarian relief program; and its potential role in propping up a totalitarian regime. A variety of other humanitarian disasters, from the Horn of Africa to the countries affected by the tsunami of 2005, have placed strains on the humanitarian system, and forced a re-evaluation of where aid will be most effectively deployed.

North Korea's food problems pose a distinctive set of challenges for the international community. In many humanitarian crises, the international community faces failed states or conflict settings that make it difficult to provide assistance. In North Korea, by contrast, the international community faces a "hard" state that has repeatedly shown a willingness to allow its population to suffer extreme deprivation. The government also tightly controls access by outsiders. Such a setting raises a number of fundamental and inter-related questions for donors, whether multilateral, bilateral, or non-governmental organizations (NGOs). Should the international community provide assistance even if it means prolonging the life of a despotic regime? Does aid prolong the very policies that led to the famine in the first place? Should donors provide assistance even if some portion of that assistance is diverted to undeserving groups, including the military and party cadre? If the decision is made to provide assistance, how can donors guarantee that food aid reaches vulnerable groups and achieves other objectives, such as inducing economic reforms or empowering new social groups?

These questions are ultimately ethical ones. It is impossible in such a setting to guarantee that all aid is being used appropriately; that is precisely why humanitarian aid to North Korea poses policy and moral dilemmas. One response to this quandary is to conclude, erroneously, that concerns over human rights and the humanitarian impulse stand in opposition. Given that human rights are meaningless in the absence of the basic sustenance required to maintain life itself, the humanitarian imperative necessarily trumps human rights concerns and requires continued engagement even where basic rights are denied. Over the longer-run, it has been argued that meeting basic economic needs provides the foundation for subsequent political development, including the granting of human and political rights.

The separation of humanitarian considerations from a human rights discourse, however, is fundamentally flawed. North Korea's tragedy has many roots, but a famine of this magnitude could only have occurred in a system in which the political leadership was insulated from events on the ground and lacking in accountability to its people. The failure of the North Korean government to guarantee adequate supplies of food to its population is inextricably linked to the government's denial of a battery of rights to its citizens: to confront public officials with their shortcomings; to publicize information that allows government officials to know the extent of distress; and to organize collectively in the face of injustice and deprivation. If these rights were present, North Korea might well have faced food shortages, but it is highly doubtful that a great famine would have occurred or that the government would be presiding over an economy characterized by chronic shortages of food.

Internationally, the closed nature of the North Korean system and the continued willingness of the North Korean regime to flout international accords impose tremendous obstacles for official and private organizations engaged in relief operations there. The absence of human rights constituted an enabling condition for the development of the famine in the first place, and has subsequently proven an obstacle to that tragedy's amelioration. The humanitarian disaster and the denial of the panoply of human, civil, and political rights cannot be meaningfully disentangled or divorced.

Yet stating these relationships does not necessarily solve the moral dilemmas facing the humanitarian community, both public and private, and the North Korean case poses problems of strategy as well as morality. How does the outside world deal with a regime that, in effect, holds its own population hostage to the humanitarian impulses of outsiders? These questions demand a careful review of what has worked in North Korea and what has not.

Background of the current food shortages and the causes of the great famine of the mid-1990s. North Korean claims that the famine was due primarily to natural disasters and external shocks are misleading in important respects. The decline in food production was visible well before the floods of 1995 but the government was slow to take the steps necessary to guarantee adequate food supplies. To attribute the famine primarily to external causes—natural or manmade—is to neglect the fundamental failure of the North Korean government to respond to its changed circumstances in a timely and appropriate way.

With plausible policy adjustments—such as maintaining food imports on commercial terms or aggressively seeking multilateral assistance—the government could have avoided the great famine and the current shortages that continue to exist. Instead, it blocked humanitarian aid to the hardest hit parts of the country during the peak of the famine and curtailed commercial imports of food as humanitarian assistance began to arrive. Rather than supplementing supply, the government has used aid largely as balance-of-payments support, cutting commercial food imports, and reallocating expenditures to other priorities, including the military.

The famine unleashed profound changes in the North Korean economy and society. The government had long criminalized a number of behaviors that households rely on during food shortages, such as travel in search of food and various forms of trade. Yet the government was unable to control these coping strategies altogether, and they contributed to a bottom-up marketization of the economy. Households came to rely on the market rather than the collapsed PDS for their food, even before the economic policy changes of 2002.

What began as a socialist famine arising out of failed agricultural policies and a misguided emphasis on self-reliance evolved into a chronic emergency more akin to those in market economies. Access to food in North Korea is no longer a function of the PDS, but of position in the market. The divide between those who could augment their wages with foreign exchange and other sources of income and those who could not has steadily widened.

The international aid effort. In confronting the fundamentally non-cooperative stance of the North Korean government, the humanitarian community has pursued two basic strategies to guarantee the integrity of its assistance: targeting of vulnerable groups, and monitoring of food deliveries to assure that these targeted populations are being reached. At virtually every point, the North Korean government has placed roadblocks in the way of the donor community, which succeeded to the extent that it did only through extraordinary perspicacity and flexibility. Yet even by its own admission, this monitoring effort is a leaky sieve, and it is estimated that between 10 and 30 percent of food aid is diverted.

Most concerns with diversion center on the appropriation of food by the military. Military and party elites have other sources of food; an equal if not greater problem is the diversion of food to the market or to less deserving groups.

Monitoring is not an end in itself—ultimately donors are concerned about the impact of relief. Again, North Korean obstructionism has hindered the development of persuasive evidence on the effects of the relief effort to date. This report examines the most recent UN-sponsored nutritional survey, as well as other evidence that has not been fully explored. This evidence includes refugee interviews, data on prices, and a consideration of the nature and evolution of access to and the distribution of food, including changes since the initiation of economic policy changes in mid-2002. The evidence is imperfect, but suggests that the crisis is by no means over, and significant segments of the population remain undernourished.

The aid process from the perspective of the donors. Despite the fact that the international community has a well-developed institutional machinery for delivering aid in the World Food Programme (WFP), humanitarian assistance is of necessity tied up with the conflicting political interests of donors. In the last several years, patience with North Korea has been waning in the United States and Japan, and overall stresses on the emergency relief system have made it harder to meet targets while multilateral aid has declined. Yet North Korea has been able to partly, if not fully, compensate for these losses by generous assistance from South Korea, increasing EU involvement, and continuing reliance on quasi-commercial imports of food and other inputs from China. These sources of aid, and particularly Chinese and South Korean assistance, are weakly monitored, if they are conditional at all, and thus reduce the ability of outsiders to press the North Korean government on issues of monitoring and transparency.

Origins of the Food Emergency

Korea was colonized by Japan in the first decade of the 20th century, and at the end of the Second World War was divided into zones of Soviet and U.S. military occupation in the North and South, respectively. Unable to agree on a formula for unification, in 1948 the Republic of Korea proclaimed sovereignty in the South and the Democratic People's Republic of Korea did the same in the North. In 1950, North Korea invaded South Korea in a bid to unify the peninsula, eventually drawing in a U.S.-dominated UN contingent in support of the South. China subsequently entered the war in support of the North. Combat ended with an armistice in 1953, with a truce line that differed little from what had been reached on the battlefield over a year before.

Historically, the northern part of the Korean peninsula was the more industrially developed and the more agrarian south was the breadbasket. With the partition of the peninsula following the Second World War, North Korea adopted a centrally planned economy along Soviet lines, and pursued the objective of food *security*—the quite understandable concern with security of supplies—through a misplaced commitment to food *self-sufficiency*, a policy of seeking to meet demand entirely through domestic production. The commitment to self-sufficiency was pursued not only at the national level, but was pushed down to the provincial, and even county level as well. Given the country's high ratio of population to

Figure 1. Sources of food supply, 1990–2003

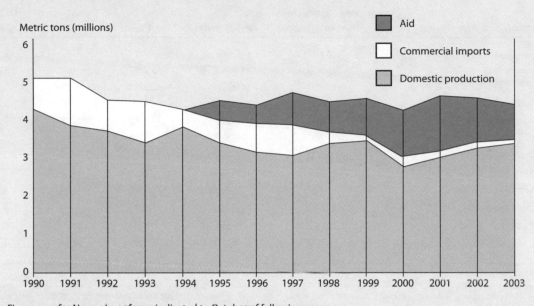

Note: Figures are for November of year indicated to October of following year.
Sources: USDA website, INTERFAIS (2004), Noland (2000)

arable land, and its relatively northern latitude and short growing seasons, this strategy proved problematic and contributed to recurrent food problems of which the present crisis is only the most recent example.

Although founding leader Kim Il Sung made *juche*, typically translated as "self-reliance," the ideological centerpiece of the regime, in fact the country relied heavily on its socialist allies for aid. The Soviet Union was the most important player, supporting the country with heavily subsidized supplies of energy, fertilizer, and manufactured products. The rapidly changing diplomatic landscape of the late Cold War period had important consequences for North Korea. As Moscow recognized South Korea and the Soviet Union collapsed, North Korea was both diplomatically isolated and cut off from important sources of concessional trade. China stepped into the breach to some extent, but it too had shifted diplomatic course and sought hard currency for its exports.

These external shocks were profound. Embroiled in a nuclear confrontation with the United States from 1992 to 1994, then undergoing a political transition with the death of Kim Il-sung just as the nuclear crisis was resolved, the leadership was slow to react. It is this failure to adjust aggressively to these fundamental geopolitical and economic changes that constitutes the root cause of the famine.

There is some disagreement about trends in production, especially with respect to the period from 1995 to 1996 when the country was hit by devastating floods. But best estimates suggest that grain output in North Korea began declining in the early 1990s (Figure 1). Because of the emphasis on self-sufficiency in food and the generally inhospitable environment for growing it, the North Korean government had developed an agricultural system that was highly dependent on a range of industrial inputs such as chemical fertilizers,

Table 1. PDS allocations and population estimates by occupation

Occupation and Age Group	Per Capita Daily Ration (grams)	Population distribution (thousands)	(%)	Ratio of Rice to Corn Pyongyang Area	Other Areas
High-ranking government officials	700	4.8	0.02	10:0	10:0
Regular laborers	600	[4905.45]	22.91	6:4	3:7
Heavy-labor workers	800	[4905.45]	22.91	6:4	3:7
Office workers	600	1976.3	9.23	6:4	3:7
Special security	800	[603.3]	2.82	7:3	7:3
Military	700	[603.3]	2.82	6:4	3:7
College students	600	591.7	2.76	6:4	3:7
Secondary school students	500	2182.5	10.19	6:4	3:7
Primary school students	400	2397.5	11.20	6:4	3:7
Preschool students	300	1270.6	5.93	6:4	3:7
Children under 3 years	100–200	1866	8.71	6:4	3:7
Aged and disabled	300	104.9	0.49	6:4	3:7

Source: Adapted from Kim, Lee, and Sumner (1998).

Note: Figures in brackets appear as such in original source to indicate that they were calculated under assumptions of the population distribution. Population figures for "Preschool students" correspond to "Children under 6 years" in original source.

insecticides, and electrically-driven irrigation systems. As the industrial economy began to implode from the withdrawal of subsidies from the Soviet Union, Russia, and then China, supply of these crucial industrial inputs fell and agricultural yields followed suit.

Food is distributed to the civilian population of North Korea through two channels. Workers on state and cooperative farms account for roughly 30 percent of the population. Most of these farmers are granted an annual allotment of grain at the time of the harvest. However, the country is highly urbanized and the bulk of the population is fed through the PDS. The PDS distributes food as a monthly or biweekly ration. Rations, in turn, vary according to occupational status as well as age. For example, high-ranking party, government, and military officials are fed through separate distribution channels and receive higher rations, as do certain classes of workers (Table 1). But occupational status, in turn, rests on political status to an important extent. Access to better jobs, party membership, and desirable residential locations, such as Pyongyang, are all affected by a complex political classification system related to family background and perceived loyalty to the regime.

As domestic output fell and the PDS was increasingly unable to fulfill its mandate, rations were cut. In 1987, rations were cut following the first reduction in Soviet assistance. In 1991, the government initiated a "let's eat two meals a day" campaign. A series of refugee surveys document that for at least some segments of the population, the PDS began failing to supply food on a regular basis—or at all—around this time. By 1994, a majority of refugees interviewed reported that the PDS had collapsed in their localities of origin (Korean Buddhist Sharing Movement 1998, Robinson et al. 1999, Robinson et al. 2001).

Careful analysis of North Korean data suggests that death rates were probably elevated by 1993, and certainly by 1994, signaling the outset of famine as typically defined. The North Korean government did step up its quest for commercial imports and made early appeals for food aid to both the United States and Japan. Yet the government was not forthcoming about the extent of distress, and these signals were mixed. As the situation deteriorated

Figure 2. North Korean food imports and aid, 1990–2003

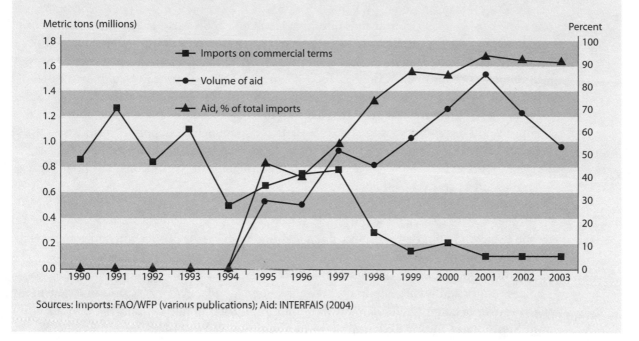

Metric tons (millions) / Percent

Legend:
- Imports on commercial terms
- Volume of aid
- Aid, % of total imports

Sources: Imports: FAO/WFP (various publications); Aid: INTERFAIS (2004)

during the lean months of the spring of 1995, the North Koreans reached out, obtaining in May a commitment from first Japan, and then South Korea, to provide emergency assistance. The first ship carrying aid to the country left port in June.

In July and August, the country experienced significant floods. The floods reflected the typical seasonal pattern of rainfall on the Korean peninsula, but they were exacerbated by the El Niño effect. However, the effects of the flood were also worsened by topsoil erosion and river silting that had followed the deforestation of hillsides as more and more marginal land was brought under cultivation to maximize output and to cope with shortages.

The floods were significant events because they provided the government a political basis for making a full-blown appeal to the international community. For example, the governmental unit that had been established to serve as the liaison with foreign donors was renamed the Flood Damage Rehabilitation Committee (FDRC), a designation that it retains to this day. Similar floods followed in 1996, and thereafter the country experienced a succession of weather-related difficulties (Woo-Cumings 2002).

There is no question that bad weather made a difficult situation worse, but it is not obvious that the floods were the primary or even proximate cause of the North Korean famine (Noland, Robinson, and Wang 2001). It is essential to place the effect of the weather in the context of two other crucial factors: the secular decline in the North Korean economy, and in the agricultural sector in particular; and the failure of the government to respond to this crisis by maintaining adequate commercial imports or by making clear and timely appeals to the international community. The decline in the economy resulted in part from external shocks, but even more fundamentally from the misguided effort to pursue a strategy of self-sufficiency, including in food. Had the government sent unambiguous signs of distress, the humanitarian community would have responded as it ultimately did. But delay in famine settings is fatal. Even well-intentioned supporters of humanitarian aid were still debating the true extent of the country's food problems as late as 1997 because of the paucity of reliable information.

If the North Korean government's refusal to reach out in the early 1990s amounted to a sin of omission, then its behavior once aid began flowing in 1996 constitutes an equally disturbing set of sins of commission. As aid began arriving, the country simultaneously moved to reduce its commercial imports of food (Figure 2). This curious feature of North Korean behavior—while the famine was continuing to take its toll—has not previously received the attention it deserves. Rather than use aid to *supplement* local production and commercial imports, aid has *substituted* for, or "crowded out," commercial imports. North Korea, in effect, has stopped importing grain through commercial routes. As a result, over the last several years more than 90 percent of the grain brought into North Korea has been in the form of aid or concessional imports.

Another way of casting these observations is in terms the government's priorities. Rather than using humanitarian assistance as an addition to domestic production and commercial sources of supply, the government has used aid largely as balance-of-payments support, allowing it to allocate the savings in commercial imports to other priorities, including military ones and luxury imports for the elite. For example, in 1999, at the same time that it was cutting commercial grain imports to less than 200,000 metric tons, the government allocated scarce foreign exchange to the purchase of 40 MiG-21 fighters and 8 military helicopters from Kazakhastan.

Moreover, one could argue that aid had another "crowding out" effect of reducing pressure to undertake reform of the agricultural sector. The failure of domestic production to return to even its 1990 level is evidence not only of the collapse of inputs, but of the halting nature of market-oriented and incentive-based reforms.

The implications of this analysis of the import behavior of the government can be seen in Figure 3, which contains estimates of minimum human demand and normal human demand derived from Food and Agricultural Organization (FAO) and WFP estimates. The Australian economist Heather Smith has pointed out that the FAO/WFP estimates (which were raised in the midst of the famine) embodied questionable assumptions both about the role of cereals in the North Korean diet and appeared to contradict the North Korean government's own historical data on grain consumption. Adjusting for either the composition of the diet (by assuming that a greater share of calories are coming from non-grain sources) or for the historical pattern of consumption in North Korea (and other Asian countries as well) generates a reduction in the minimum human needs target of roughly 20 percent (Smith 1998).

As can be seen in Figure 3, the minimum human-needs target, adjusted or unadjusted, was met in every year, at least casting doubt on whether the North Korean famine was the result of an absolute lack of food. Indeed, the much higher normal human needs target that embodies a "normal" level of consumption beyond survival needs, was met half the time during the early and mid-1990s, even as the famine was cresting. It is only from the late-1990s to the present that actual aggregate food supplies have not met normal human demands. The reason for this appears clear from the calculations conducted for this report: commercial imports collapse.

Figure 3 reports two counterfactual supply lines—the first is what would have been aggregate supply if commercial imports had stayed at their 1993 levels and North Korea had aid.

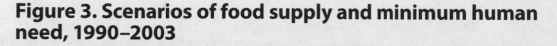

Figure 3. Scenarios of food supply and minimum human need, 1990–2003

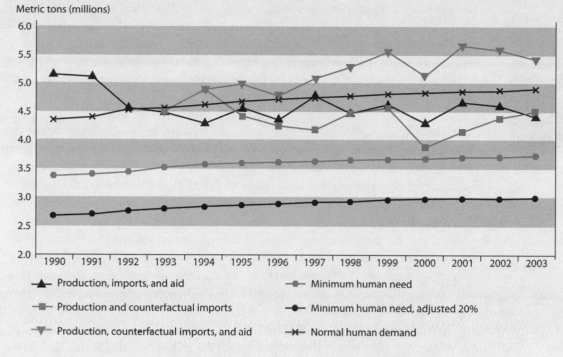

Metric tons (millions)

Legend:
- ▲ Production, imports, and aid
- ■ Production and counterfactual imports
- ▼ Production, counterfactual imports, and aid
- ■ Minimum human need
- ● Minimum human need, adjusted 20%
- ✕ Normal human demand

Note: Demand figures based on population data taken from the Bank of Korea and annual per capita consumption of 167kg in cereal equivalent. Counterfactual supply keeps 1994-2003 imports held at 1993 level.
Sources: Production: USDA website; Imports: Noland (2003), INTERFAIS (2004).

This may be an excessively optimistic scenario. If North Korea had maintained commercial imports it may have received less aid. The second counterfactual supply line depicts what aggregate supply would have been if commercial imports had remained at 1993 levels and the international community had provided North Korea with *no* aid. These present the limiting cases; the likely outcome would have fallen in-between.

In Figure 3, the first counterfactual supply line exceeds the unadjusted normal human demand target in every year. Even the unduly pessimistic second counterfactual line—true self-reliance—exceeds the minimum human needs line in every year.

To these policy failures and the priorities revealed by the government's import behavior must be added a third crucial determinant of the extent of the famine. As the situation worsened in the mid-1990s, the northern and eastern parts of the country were left to fend for themselves. Due to high urbanization and inhospitable growing conditions, these regions were food-deficit areas, dependent on shipments from other parts of the country. As supplies from these parts of the country dwindled, and the transportation system broke down due to lack of fuel, the government proved unable, or unwilling, to meet the needs of this part of the country. The government blocked external assistance targeted to the East Coast by initially limiting the access of external monitors, even as refugee interviews were revealing clear signs of growing desperation.

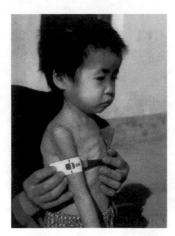

In contrast to most famines, North Korea's was an urban as well as rural phenomenon. Those rural areas that were directly affected by the floods and droughts clearly suffered, as they lost both production and stocks and were not provisioned by the government. But farmers had opportunities to hoard and divert food and to cultivate private plots. City dwellers were almost completely dependent on the PDS. Pyongyang—the seat of government and of the ruling elite—was at least relatively protected, although even there, households experienced shortages. But the large industrial cities in North and South Hamgyong, as well as smaller county seats, were particularly hard hit. As is always the case, food shortages took a particularly heavy toll on vulnerable groups such as children and the elderly.

Assessing the ultimate impact of the famine is impeded by the closed nature of the North Korean system, which forecloses access to official data and the normal channels of academic inquiry. Estimates of the death toll vary widely from the North Korean government's quasi-official figure of 220,000 to an estimate of 3.5 million by the South Korean NGO Good Friends Center for Peace, Human Rights, and Refugees (Good Friends 2004). Lacking direct access to domestic residents, analysts are forced to project onto the entire population information derived from a limited and possibly unrepresentative sample of refugees. A team from the Johns Hopkins School of Public Health working from 771 refugee interviews carefully constructed mortality rates for what was by consensus the single worst affected province (North Hamgyong) and estimated that between nearly 12 percent of the province's population had died (Robinson et al. 1999). Extrapolating this mortality rate to the whole country (something the Johns Hopkins team is careful not to do) would yield an estimate of more than 2.6 million deaths, which is almost certainly too high. More recently, two groups of analysts working independently (indeed, unbeknownst to each other) using somewhat different data and more sophisticated methodologies have come to remarkably similar estimates that seem more plausible. These studies suggest between 600,000 and 1 million excess deaths, or roughly 3–5 percent of the pre-crisis population (Goodkind and West 2000, Lee 2003). As in other famines, most of these excess deaths were not due to starvation per se. As caloric intake falls, immune systems weaken and people typically succumb to diseases such as tuberculosis before starving to death; both the young and the old are particularly vulnerable in this regard.

Even with these reduced estimates of fatalities, the North Korean famine ranks as one of the most devastating of the century and certainly the worst of the last twenty years. Moreover, these estimates do not consider births foregone through miscarriages, stillbirths, and reduced incidence of conception, which typically account for a significant component of the demographic impact of famine. Nor do they capture long-term developmental damage to survivors, and particularly to infants suffering from poor prenatal and perinatal nutrition.

To recap, the food situation in North Korea began to deteriorate in the early 1990s, as the government proved unable or unwilling to manage the external shocks associated with the changing terms of Soviet and Chinese trade, the dissolution of the former Soviet Union, and the collapse of the Russian and Eastern European economies (which had also been mainstays of support). Mortality rates were rising by 1994, if not earlier. By the spring of 1995 the situation had grown sufficiently desperate that the government approached first Japan, then South Korea, to obtain emergency assistance that was granted. In the summer, the country was hit by floods. This chronology is important: the worsening food situation and the onset of famine *preceded* the natural disasters that were real, but of secondary importance.

Figure 4. Estimates of daily per capita PDS rations

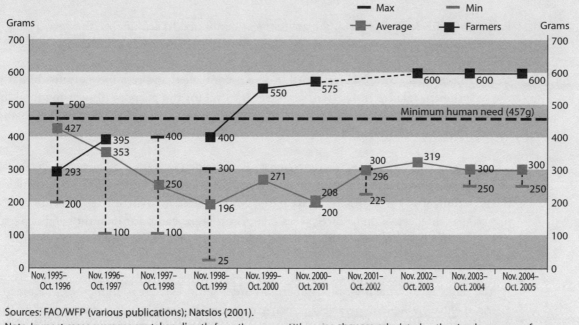

Sources: FAO/WFP (various publications); Natsios (2001).

Note: In most cases averages are taken directly from the source. Otherwise, they are calculated as the simple average of the estimates for different cohorts throughout the marketing year.

The North Korean government subsequently attributed the famine to natural disasters—floods and drought—and indirectly to the decline in preferential trade relations with fraternally allied socialist states. This exculpation is misleading. The change in North Korea's external economic relations was clearly permanent, not merely a transitory shock, and the decline in food production was visible well before the floods of 1995. Yet the government was slow to recognize the extent of the problem and take the steps necessary to guarantee adequate food supplies. To attribute the famine primarily to external causes is to neglect the fundamental failure of the government to respond to its changed circumstances in a timely and appropriate way. By maintaining the level of commercial food imports or aggressively seeking humanitarian assistance, the government could have avoided the famine and the current shortages that continue to exist. Times would have been tough in North Korea during the 1990s under almost any policy, but a famine killing three to five percent of the population was not pre-ordained. The sustained pursuit of ineffectual and perverse policies that allowed this tragedy to transpire could only have occurred in a setting where the famine's victims were denied political voice. The North Korean famine and the country's failure to protect basic human rights are inseparable.

Post-famine Changes:
Control, Marketization, Reform

The famine had profound consequences for North Korean society. Families were forced into coping behaviors such as gathering wild foods, selling assets, and engaging in various forms of petty trade, barter, and illicit exchange. Markets sprung up not only as a matter of policy, but as households bartered goods or whatever could be stripped from places of employment for food that had been illicitly diverted from cooperative farms and hidden plots.

Faced with this loss of control, the government continued to criminalize the very coping strategies that allowed people to survive and even added new controls. During famines, people travel, either to relocate to a destination where conditions are less severe, or to trade. However, all travel within North Korea is controlled and requires permits. Initially, the government relaxed restrictions on internal travel for the purpose of securing food, but undocumented movement remained illegal and thus vulnerable to low-level extortion and corruption (Good Friends 2000).

The fundamental right to leave one's country is enshrined in both the Universal Declaration of Human Rights and the International Covenant on Civil and Political Rights to which the government of the DPRK is a state party. Nonetheless, the North Korean penal code prescribes sentences of up to three years in a prison-labor camp for unauthorized departure. These camps are characterized by extreme deprivation, torture, and high rates of death while in detention (Hawk 2003).

As the ranks of internal migrants and cross-border refugees increased, the North Korean government responded in a variety of ways, including by establishing a network of ad hoc detention facilities, again, characterized by extreme deprivation, torture, and in the case of pregnant women repatriated from China, forced abortions and infanticide (Hawk 2003). Adults engaged in illegal internal movement and famine-orphaned children (the *kotjebis* or "wandering sparrows") were subject to detention in so-called "9-27 camps" named after the date (September 27, 1995) when North Korean leader Kim Jong Il issued the edict authorizing their establishment. Men over 16 who had crossed the border were vulnerable to incarceration in prison-labor camps and long-term political prison camps that constitute the North Korean gulag.

The collapse of the social compact in the 1990s and the bottom-up marketization of the economy carried at least the promise of a sector of the economy outside state control. But this marketization suffered from the absence of legal foundations or institutions, and was undertaken in the context of macroeconomic instability that has spawned its own set of problems. What began as a socialist famine arising out of failed agricultural policies, a misguided emphasis on self-reliance, and the collapse of the PDS, evolved into a chronic emergency more akin to those observed in market economies. Access to food was increasingly a function of the ability to command resources in the market. Again, the urban population found itself at a great disadvantage in this setting.

During the great famine of the mid-1990s, the PDS proved unable to provide even the minimal amount of food needed for human survival. What is striking, however, is that this system of distribution has never fully revived. Figure 4 shows the data on average rations distributed through the PDS since 1995. These averages hide important variations across provinces and over time, and in recent months there is evidence that the situation has deteriorated (Brooke 2005). Seasonal variations are particularly important; as recently as 2001, PDS distributions dropped sharply during the "lean months" of spring. But the larger picture is still striking. Even after the famine, and with the tremendous multilateral aid effort, the PDS currently distributes less than 350 grams of food per person daily, well short of the 450 grams deemed an absolute minimum caloric intake.

The flip side of this observation is that households out of necessity are securing a larger share of their food through the market, including general markets in larger cities, farmers' markets, and more informal markets or exchange networks (such as barter, transfers from relatives in the countryside, and corruption). A simple balance sheet approach that weighs total domestic production, imports, and aid against food distributed through the PDS suggests that over the past five years most of domestic production (less on-farm consumption) has probably gone into the market. The PDS has increasingly become a mechanism for distributing aid. Total aid receipts are equal to roughly three-quarters of the food that North Korean authorities claim is being distributed through the PDS.

Sunam Market in Chongjin where international food aid is sold.

This declining reliance of households on the PDS is confirmed by a series of refugee surveys done by several different researchers (Robinson et al. 1999, 2001; Good Friends 1998, 2000; Chang, forthcoming). They paint a consistent story: The PDS ceased to deliver food to large segments of the population in the mid-1990s, and families were forced to adopt a variety of coping strategies to survive. A recent survey of nearly 1,000 refugees in China confirms the marginality of the PDS system for many people.

In July 2002, the government undertook policy changes that seemed to ratify, or at least de-criminalize, the implicit marketization that had been occurring for years. This is not the venue to go into a detailed analysis of these policy changes, but they have proved problematic in both design and implementation. The WFP has begun to conduct household surveys and canvass local officials, and as result has been gathering more detailed information on the effects of the reforms. These studies conclude that the steep industrial decline that began in the 1990s continues to this day. Many factories are running well under capacity, and as a consequence as much as 30 percent of the workforce outside of agriculture may be unemployed. Among those who remain employed in the industrial sector, there is considerable underemployment, and some workers who continue to receive salaries have seen their wages cut by 50 to 80 percent in real terms. Women appear to be particularly affected by these developments with an unemployment rate double that of men.

A second aspect of the reforms was a large administrative increase in official prices and wages. The price increases were designed in part to ratify the emergence of market prices that were far higher than official ones; the wage increase was designed to offset these price increases and thus to maintain real incomes at least to some extent. Yet the lack of revival of industrial sector production and the authorities' decision to monetize the fiscal costs of subsidies to loss-making state-owned industrial enterprises has meant too many *won* chasing too few products. The result has been a high, sustained inflation that is estimated at more than 100 percent annually since August 2002.

As the market has come to supply a greater and greater share of total consumption and as prices have begun to spiral up, a new divide has appeared in North Korean society. On the one side are those who can augment their wages with foreign exchange, which at least partly insulates its holders from the effects of ongoing inflation and other sources of income. Farmers have also probably done reasonably well as a result of rising food prices, although it is difficult to be sure. On the other side are those households, mostly urban, who lived on shrinking local currency wages and lack access to foreign exchange, other income-earning opportunities, or alternative sources of food such as family connections in the countryside or abroad. Food prices have risen far faster than nominal wages, resulting in a sharp decline in the welfare of those forced to purchase food in the market. The most disturbing implication of this growing marketization is the creation of a "new poor," with the cities once again being severely affected. What began as a socialist famine has evolved into an entitlement food emergency, with position in the market a crucial determinant of access to food.

According to WFP surveys, households dependent on the PDS—overwhelmingly in the cities and towns—spend roughly one-third of their income on PDS-supplied food alone. A typical family of four with one income would spend 40 percent of its budget on PDS-supplied food. Some households surveyed by the WFP report spending 50 to 60 percent of their household incomes on PDS food. However, recall that in many areas and time periods, the PDS is supplying households with only one half of an absolute minimum caloric need, and in some cases less than that. If these households are nonetheless spending one-third of their incomes on PDS food, this leaves only one-third of their budgets to cover remaining caloric needs through other sources, needs that are as high as half of minimum requirements. Market prices are conventionally thought to be three or more times higher than PDS prices even after the price reforms raised the prices charged to consumers through the PDS. As a result, WFP surveys are finding that some households are spending up to 80 percent of their income on food, inclusive of non-PDS sources.

How do households cope? What is striking is the continuity in coping behaviors between the high famine period and the current setting, despite a massive increase in food aid. According to the WFP, 40 percent of interviewed households report receiving food from relatives in rural areas. Sixty to 80 percent of PDS-dependent (i.e., urban) households and 65 percent of cooperative farm households report gathering wild foods. Many households and workplaces maintain "kitchen gardens" and, as in other cases of economic stress around the world, there are extensive anecdotal reports of households selling or bartering personal belongings for food and engaging in other socially disruptive coping behaviors, including crime, human trafficking, and prostitution.

According to the WFP, households with a single earner and dependents and PDS-dependent households without access to "kitchen gardens" are the most vulnerable. The targeting strategy of the WFP may also miss important segments of the vulnerable population. For example, households with children—a targeted group—may benefit from the supplementary rations provided through institutions. But households without children that are not participating in food-for-work programs would not receive any benefit from aid, except indirectly through its effect on market prices.

The reality may be even worse. One interpretation of the price increases, as noted previously, is that they were simply bringing PDS food prices in line with the market. Yet there is also anecdotal evidence that even the pretense of universalism has been breached. Recent reports suggest that the authorities have significantly reduced the number of households being issued PDS ration cards. These anecdotal reports are fully consistent with the most recent refugee surveys. One such survey finds that less than 4 percent of the refugees interviewed "agreed" or "strongly agreed" with the statement that there had been an improvement in food availability since the July 2002 policy changes were enacted. Moreover, 85 percent of these refugees, who admittedly may not be representative of the country as a whole, "agreed" or "strongly agreed" with the statement that North Koreans are voicing their opinions about the chronic food shortage (Chang, forthcoming).

In sum, although the period of high famine has passed, North Korea continues to experience chronic food shortages that are hitting hard at an underemployed and unemployed urban working class in particular. Targeting children is important but insufficient; many vulnerable households are not on the target list. Moreover, given the political stratification of North Korea and the inability of the WFP to achieve minimum standards of transparency and monitoring in its operations, deserving households—including politically disfavored households—are not getting the food intended for them or are being denied relief altogether.

Obtaining better information through baseline surveys and focus groups would be invaluable in gaining a better understanding of what is happening in North Korea, and the WFP and the U.S. Agency for International Development (USAID) are making efforts in this regard. But better information alone will not significantly improve the effectiveness of the humanitarian effort in North Korea. To see why requires a more thorough consideration of the issues of monitoring and diversion of food aid.

The Issues of Monitoring and Diversion

After nearly a decade of relief efforts, North Korean practices still fall well below international norms with respect to transparency and non-discrimination in the distribution of humanitarian relief.

During the postwar period, the public humanitarian relief system centered on the UN agencies, particularly on the WFP, which has developed a well-articulated set of norms governing the implementation of relief operations. At the core of these norms are principles of non-discrimination and distribution based on need: "priority in food aid should be given to the most vulnerable populations" and "such aid should be based on the needs of the intended beneficiaries." The notion of non-discrimination is defined with respect to age, gender, social status, ethnicity, and political beliefs (Ziegler 2002).

These basic norms, as well as basic principles of accountability within donor countries, drive the related insistence on thorough monitoring of aid, which is codified in the WFP handbook in a standard operating procedure embodying reciprocal obligations on the parts of donors and recipients. There have been parallel attempts to codify norms within the NGO community, including prior understanding of basic conditions; evaluation of effectiveness; participation by recipients in the design, management, and monitoring of programs; distribution of aid through a transparent system that can be monitored and adequately audited; and impartiality or the distribution of aid in a fair and equitable manner (Sphere 2004).

The desire to articulate clear norms among the humanitarian community is not simply an exercise in idealism; it is also designed to solve a particular set of incentive problems that can emerge in any humanitarian operation. In the absence of normative constraints, the differences among donors and competition among them can lead to a "race to the bottom": a willingness to turn a blind eye toward diversion; a tendency to exaggerate aid effectiveness; and even the empowerment of groups who bear responsibility for causing the humanitarian crisis in the first place.

In this context, it should be observed that the practices of two of the major donors, China and South Korea, ignore international humanitarian norms. The terms governing China's shipment of grain and other major foodstuffs is largely opaque, but the country makes no pretense of targeting vulnerable populations or monitoring. Indeed, the apparent Chinese practice of providing food directly to the North Korean military is reputedly undertaken so

Hyesan Market, Yanggang Province.

that the North Koreans can claim that multilateral aid does not go to the military. South Korea's practices are only marginally better: donations go directly into the PDS and monitoring is minimal. A number of South Korean NGOs have complained repeatedly that food is channeled to undeserving groups, in ratios that may be as high as 50 percent (Good Friends 2005).

In this context, it is also important to be clear on the meaning of diversion, a term that is used casually and has multiple meanings. The most common image is of the military seizing grain to feed the army and party cadre. But the political and military elite has a variety of channels for accessing food, including "first draw" on the domestic harvest, access to imports from China and South Korea that are weakly monitored or not monitored at all, and access to grain and other foods via the market through privileged access to foreign exchange.

This type of diversion is no doubt real, but almost certainly exaggerated. Much less attention has been given to the effect of the huge difference between controlled and market prices on the incentive to divert food for *economic* reasons: to sell it in the market. These incentives operate with respect to farmers—who can earn more by selling to the market than surrendering grain to the state—and they almost certainly operate with respect to aid as well. Local military and political officials and those involved in the transport of grain have strong incentives to divert aid to non-deserving groups or to the market.

Since its early operations in the country, the WFP has sought to address this problem through two means: (1) devising lists of target groups, and (2) selective monitoring of the institutions and programs—such as food-for-work programs—through which aid is delivered to recipients. Public distribution centers (PDCs) are the main channel for the delivery of food to the general, non-targeted population. These centers can be thought of as final "retail" outlets, where households purchase prescribed amounts of food using ration cards. The primary channel for delivering food to targeted groups is via more than 40,000 institutions such as schools, orphanages, and hospitals.

However, there is no separate channel in North Korea for distributing food to these institutions; food passes through the same county-level PDS warehouse before it is distributed to the final units. These county-level warehouses are controlled by People's Committees made up of mid-level government and party officials. These groups confront multiple demands on the food they control, from central authorities wishing to reallocate the food regionally, to local military and work units, to outright corruption.

Addressing the problem of diversion is particularly difficult in North Korea because even the most basic international norms are not observed. In essence, there exists a fundamental lack of trust between the government of North Korea and the international donor community. Indicative of this stance is the fact that Jean Ziegler, UN Special Rapporteur on the Right to Food, has been denied entry to North Korea five times, despite the fact that UN programs have been feeding nearly one-third of the population on an ongoing basis.

For nearly a decade, the North Korean government has consistently violated its fundamental obligation to facilitate WFP activities within the country. NGOs have been subject to similar obstacles, though given the sheer diversity of NGOs operating in North Korea some have been more successful in handling these constraints than others. There have been marginal improvements in access over time, but these have been grudging and have had a two-steps-forward, one-step-back character. What follows is meant to outline the basic constraints on project design, implementation, and monitoring. The characterization below should neither be interpreted as holding universally (some of the smaller NGOs may have effectively negotiated better access terms), nor necessarily holding at every moment in time since 1995. Where there have been recent improvements in practice, these are noted. However, it characterizes broadly the de facto monitoring regime for the single major channel of food to North Korea, the WFP.

With respect to basic issues of program design, the North Korean government imposes restrictions on the activities of the WFP and other groups that fundamentally inhibit the implementation of rational famine-relief programs:

- With respect to the NGOs, the North Korean government routinely denies visas in the absence of a pre-commitment to a target aid level, making pre-delivery assessment or program design difficult, if not impossible.

- The WFP and other groups have been denied access to parts of the country—parts of the country believed to be particularly vulnerable. When the aid effort first began, aid was denied to whole provinces on the East Coast. After 1997, these restrictions were eased, but since 2000 there have been only marginal improvements in the number of counties to which the WFP has access, and 42 of 203 counties in the country remain off limits. As a result, the WFP has no information on the food situation in these restricted areas.

- The WFP and others generally do not have access to markets where food is sold, even though information on market prices is indispensable to understanding the distribution of food.

Once a program has been agreed upon, the donor must recruit staff to implement it. With the exception of the South Korean government effort, which has only a minimal monitoring regime, official relief agencies are not permitted to use Korean speakers or ethnic Korean staff. In the case of NGOs, the North Korean government has been reluctant in granting visas to Korean speakers, though this is not uniformly the case. In 2004, the North Korean government allowed resident WFP staff to begin Korean-language lessons.

- Without Korean speakers, the WFP and other organizations are reliant on government-supplied interpreters who owe their primary allegiance to the Flood Damage Rehabilitation Committee (FDRC), not the relief agency that pays their salary.

- In the case of the NGOs, the North Korean government has shown reluctance to issue long-term visas. For example, NGOs planning to deliver aid for five months were given two-month visas and the government has denied issuance of multiple-entry visas.

- The WFP has faced constant North Korean opposition to its desired number of monitors.

- Agency staffing levels are contingent on the dollar value of aid. Operational protocols specifically reflect this and if donations drop, staff members are asked to leave.

- The government restricts the use of vehicles and requires the use of FDRC-seconded drivers. Travel outside Pyongyang requires pre-approval (typically a week or more in advance) and accompaniment by official escorts or "minders." Not until April 2002 could WFP sub-office employees outside Pyongyang walk outside their hotels without being accompanied.

American food aid sold in Sunam Market. On the bag it reads "Gift from the U.S."

The implications of the inability to recruit, train, and maintain authority over local staff should not be underestimated. As one observer put it, "their reporting loyalties are almost always toward the government" (Bennett 1999). One aid worker described a situation that would be amusing if not for the stakes. Unable to speak Korean or read Korean language signs, the aid workers had no idea if they were being shown the institutions that they had requested to visit, and in one instance suspected that they had been taken to the same institution twice. Even if humanitarian organizations are not worried about their North Korean counterparts "cheating" them, North Korea's insistence on staffing these positions with people trained as translators undermines effectiveness. As Dammers, Fox, and Jimenez (2005) observe, of the UN Children's Fund's (UNICEF) ten North Korean counterparts, none have specific technical or sectoral skills.

Once a program is initiated, North Korean practices make it impossible for the WFP or non-resident NGOs working through its Food Aid Liaison Unit (FALU) to track relief shipments from port to recipient. The opportunities for leakage in such a system are multiple. Typically the WFP and NGOs rely on a paper trail of transport waybills and transaction receipts at local PDCs to track supplies. Major diversion at the port is unlikely, but much food does not go from port to truck but rather to trains and barges before it is transferred to trucks; these shipments are not tracked. Relief officials have at times expressed the view that these records were fabricated, though whether this was done to hide diversion or as the result of simple lack of administrative capacity is unclear. There have also been a number of eyewitness accounts by foreigners, as well as refugee and defector testimonies to outright diversion by military units, though whether this was part of a centrally directed conspiracy or simply opportunistic behavior by local commanders is also unknown.

Once food reaches the county warehouse, the only check on delivery to the final institutional destinations—whether PDCs or targeted institutions—and on the use made of the food by those final destinations is through spot checks by WFP sub-offices. Although large-scale diversion at higher stages in the distribution chain is possible, it is at this lower level that monitoring is necessarily the weakest and diversion thus most likely to occur. The magnitude of the task of tracking supplies across tens of thousands of end-user institutions under abysmal working conditions should not be underestimated. Ironically, some NGOs, operating on a vastly smaller scale may actually have a more accurate grasp of where their contributions are ending up, despite the fact that they undertake less rigorous monitoring.

The behavior of these county-level institutions is difficult to characterize, but numerous accounts provide revealing information on what are certainly larger patterns. Dammers, Fox, and Jimenez (2005) reported on an EU-funded UNICEF program that distributes therapeutic milk, a product that can be fatal if administered incorrectly. According to the 2003/2004 agreement, the milk was to be provided to three provincial hospitals with properly-trained staff. However during a monitoring visit in November 2003, the EU's technical assistant discovered that the supplies were being distributed to baby-homes in the cities of Hyesan and Chongjin. The North Korean government then proposed for the 2004/2005 cycle that the product be distributed to 157 rehabilitation centers of various sorts, an alteration in terms of reference that Dammers, Fox, and Jimenez describe as without justification, cost-ineffective, and potentially dangerous. These diverted supplies did not disappear into the ether: they were consumed, but not by the intended beneficiaries.

This example is a small-scale one, but there are suggestions that much larger-scale diversion from intended purpose is occurring. Good Friends, a South Korean organization with long involvement with the issue, estimates that as much as 50 percent of Korean aid is going to non-deserving groups, including the military. In a particularly interesting development in 2004, the WFP reported that county authorities were buying and selling grain among themselves (WFP 2004). In all of these cases, humanitarian assistance is being consumed; the issue is not one of a deadweight or total loss. But donors have very little control, and aid is undoubtedly going to less deserving groups and therefore bypassing or only indirectly affecting targeted, vulnerable populations.

On the bags it reads "White Rice CARITAS."

Given norms of accountability among donors and the limits on staffing resources even under the best of circumstances, the integrity of relief efforts are typically maintained through random, unannounced inspections. The North Korean government imposes restrictions on operations that make satisfactory monitoring of implementation and effectiveness through this means almost impossible:

- The North Korean government still has not provided a comprehensive list of institutions that benefit from WFP support despite repeated requests over a period of years.

- Pre-notification is required and visits to specific sites may be denied. The standard procedure is for the WFP to make weekly requests to visit facilities in particular regions that North Korean authorities review. In 2002, about eight percent of requests were denied. By 2003, this had fallen to one percent. WFP officials claim that they can increase the effective "randomness" embodied in this procedure, for example, by proposing to visit an orphanage in a particular county (of which there are, say, seven) and on visitation day demand to be taken to a particular orphanage of the seven possible.

- Interviewees at any given site cannot be chosen at random and the WFP is not allowed to interview households that are not already receiving aid—thus undercutting their ability to assess whether aid is going to the most needy or allocated on a politically discriminatory basis.

- When making monitoring visits, WFP staff are accompanied not only by local officials—who may be quite sympathetic to WFP concerns—but by FDRC staff as well. Given the rigidly authoritarian nature of the political system, the presence of representatives of the central government stifles the creation of alliances and networks with local officials or the revelation of any information that may be unflattering to the government.

In December 1996, North Korean leader Kim Jong Il allegedly gave a speech commemorating the founding of Kim Il Sung University that was transcribed and smuggled out of the country. The speech is a wide-ranging review of the problems the country faced at the time, including the food problem. In it, Kim Jong Il admits that lower-level party and administrative officials had sought to mislead him about actual conditions on the ground. If Kim Jong Il himself has been unable to solve this fundamental information problem, is there reason to believe that the WFP will be more successful?

What appears to be at work is not centrally directed conspiracies (though these may exist), but rather local politics. The county-level administrators, who have enormous influence over the disposition of supplies, have a number of conflicting motivations, ranging from genuine desire to reach targeted groups and distribute food equally, to sincere differences with donors over priorities, to the universal phenomenon of local political "back-scratching," to personal pecuniary gain from diversion. The latter is undoubtedly important when considering that these mid-level government and party officials are themselves living on rapidly eroding *won*-denominated salaries.

How large is this diversion, and what effect does it have? No one knows for sure, but it is likely to be substantial. Good Friends recently estimated that as much as half of aid is diverted in the sense of going to non-targeted, privileged groups (Good Friends 2005).[2] Extensive interviews with a number of people affiliated with official and non-governmental organizations involved with humanitarian relief operations in North Korea who have intimate knowledge of the operations of their respective organizations, both public and private, yielded estimates of diversion that ranged from 10 percent to 30 percent. These estimates are significant, though well below the Good Friends figure. If one accepts the notion that there have been improvements in monitoring in recent years, then it could well be the case that losses were even higher in the past.

Some indirect evidence can be adduced from refugee surveys. One of the most astonishing things to come out of one recent survey of nearly 1,000 refugees is the relative absence of self-reported receipt of aid (Chang, forthcoming). Only 63 percent of the respondents in this survey reported even knowing of the *existence* of foreign humanitarian assistance. Ten years into the humanitarian effort, nearly 40 percent of the population remains unaware of the aid effort, despite the fact that it purports to target virtually all of the school-aged children in the country. Of those who knew of the program, only seven percent reported having received aid (or less than five percent of the total sample including those who were unaware of aid deliveries). These numbers do not imply that only seven percent of the population received aid, nor do they constitute proof of diversion. They do, however, testify to the extraordinary power of the government to control information. When asked who respondents thought were the primary recipients of aid, fully 98 percent responded "the military." Again, these responses do not prove that the military has been the primary recipient of food aid, but they are powerful testimony to North Korean views of how food is distributed in the country.

After the tragic train explosion in Ryongchon in April 2004, members of the international community responded by sending food and medical aid to North Korea. In July 2004, a Japanese NGO obtained video footage of Sunam Market in Chongjin where some of this aid was being sold. The video contains conversations between the recorder of the film and the vendors in the market.

Sunam Market, Chongjin, July 2004
"Conversation 1"

Vendor: Buy some rice.
Recorder: The quality of rice seems good.
Vendor: It is the rice from the recent aid.
Recorder: From where?
Vendor: From aid to Ryongchon. I went all the way to Ryongchon to get this rice.
Recorder: Oh, that's why it's expensive.

To get a rough sense of the magnitude of the estimates of diversion, the humanitarian effort organized by the WFP has aspired to provide at least a minimum ration to approximately 30 percent of the North Korean populace in recent years. If the estimate cited above is correct, it implies that the diversion of aid is sufficient to feed a significant share of the North Korean people. In light of the high real price of food in North Korea, and the astronomical rents that could be reaped through diversion, those who manage to get control of these supplies have a strong pecuniary incentive to both maintain the aid program, from where they derive their profits, and escape detection.

In the presence of markets, the welfare effects of diversion are ambiguous, however. Diversion directly moves food away from intended beneficiaries. But food is fungible to an important degree. To the extent that the recipients of diverted aid substitute it for food that they would have otherwise purchased, diversion

---

[2] Their report claims that 30 percent of food aid goes to the military, 10 percent to special organizations, 10 percent to major factories and workplaces, and the remaining 50 percent to general distribution through PDCs, although it does not explain how these estimates are reached. Note that this estimate contains no direct diversion to the market per se.

tends to depress prices in the market where many of the beneficiaries or their families are, in reality, obtaining most of their food. Again, we know this because neither North Korean nor WFP estimates of daily PDS rations are sufficient to meet even the minimum caloric intake, even if corrections are made for the presence of other types of foods besides grains.

U.S. and South Korean rice being sold in Sunam Market, Chongjin. The rice bags are not yet opened.

■ This analysis leads to an important policy conclusion. In addition to gaining better access to the PDS, outside monitors should be tracking developments in markets, where signs of food distress often appear first as wildly fluctuating grain prices.

Is further progress likely? The record over the last year has been mixed. On one hand, more of the WFP's requests for monitoring visits have been denied than in the past. The total number of visits by WFP monitors has been reduced by roughly 40 percent, and North Korean authorities have restricted the nature of questions that the WFP can pose in their focus groups. Although a handful of previously closed counties were reopened, there is still 17 percent of the population of the country living in counties that are closed to inspectors.

On the other hand, the focus groups and more detailed questionnaires have provided an important window on household behavior. The WFP also appears to have reached an agreement in principle with the North Korean government to introduce a number of changes in the monitoring regime, including baseline surveys, closer monitoring of distribution centers and food-for-work projects, and the issue of new ration cards. The WFP is also discussing the introduction of modern inventory-management systems that would allow the WFP to track individual bags of grain electronically. If implemented, these changes would improve the monitoring climate, perhaps even substantially. However, they would probably still leave it short of standard humanitarian principles in some important respects, including most notably the small number of expatriate staff allowed in-country.

Measuring Effectiveness

Much emphasis in the humanitarian and human rights community is placed on the integrity of monitoring. It is often assumed that if the monitoring system worked properly, better outcomes would follow. Yet a second way of gauging effectiveness is to look at surveys of health status. Unfortunately, precious little evidence exists on the actual impact of relief. UN-sponsored nutrition surveys that have been done to date, however, can be evaluated, as can a variety of other sorts of evidence that has not been fully explored in this context. This evidence includes refugee interviews, data on prices, and a consideration of the nature and evolution of access to and the distribution of food, including changes since the initiation of economic policy changes in mid-2002.[3] With the usual caveats about the quality of information that the North Koreans allow outsiders to collect, one conclusion is clear: Although there has been some marginal improvement in nutritional status since the peak of the famine, the crisis is by no means over and any discussion of what to do about North Korea must begin by recognizing that the fundamental problem of food insecurity has not been solved.

The UN has supported a series of nutritional surveys, the most recent of which was conducted in 2004. The North Koreans impose severe constraints on the implementation of these surveys. The most recent one, for example, does not cover all of the counties the WFP

---

[3] There have been only very limited private attempts to evaluate nutritional status or aid effectiveness. Some of these efforts are discussed in Korea Development Institute (1999).

Table 2. Regional price differences

(North Korean *won*) Item	Pyongyang August 2004	Chongjin, Northern Hamgyong August 26, 2004
Rice (1kg)	420 (imported)*	900
Corn (1kg)	200	450 - 480
Cooking oil (bean oil 1 kg)	1,500	2,000
Egg (hen, 1 egg)	45	100
Pork (1 kg)	1,000	2,700
Sugar (1 kg)	470	900
Exchange Rate	1 Euro: 2,000	1,300 (unofficial)

*The actual price of North Korean rice in Tongilgeori General Market was 680 *won* per kg.

Source: Sung-wook Nam. *Future Prospects of North Korean July Economic Reform and Implication from the Perspective of Comparative Socialism,* p. 15.

serves. The methodologies employed leave much to be desired, and questions remain about the accuracy of the reported results. Moreover, because of differences in the methodologies and populations studied in successive surveys, it is difficult to draw strong conclusions about trends over time. Nonetheless, these surveys provide a stark portrait of the food and nutritional situation of the most vulnerable populations in North Korea, including particularly children.

At the national level, the rate of stunting (measured height-for-age), signaling chronic malnutrition, was found to be 37 percent among children under the age of six. The underweight share (measured weight-for-age) was 23 percent. Wasting, a measure of acute malnutrition (measured weight-for height) was 7 percent. The share of the undernourished in North Korea's population puts it in the worst-off category in a recent FAO study, in the company of the very poorest countries including Sierra Leone, Ethiopia, and Haiti (FAO 2004).

The survey revealed considerable regional variation. For example, the stunting rate in Pyongyang (26 percent) was well below that in the eastern provinces of South Hamgyong (47 percent) and Yanggang (46 percent); similar results were found with respect to those found to be underweight, and even larger differences existed with respect to wasting. This evidence is consistent with the historical record, which indicates that privileged areas such as Pyongyang fare much better than more remote mountainous areas of the north and above all the cities and towns of the eastern provinces.

This mixed assessment of progress does *not* mean that delivered aid is ineffective; although these levels of malnutrition are still acute, they show some improvement from the peak of the famine. But they demonstrate the uphill battle the humanitarian community must fight in a context where other features of the system make it difficult to be effective. Just as the closed nature of the North Korean system inhibits effective program design, implementation, and monitoring, it prevents effective evaluation as well. In particular, the evidence from the nutrition surveys shows very important regional differences. Considerable food price dispersion across regions also indicates that while the process of marketization is well under way, markets remain fragmented (Table 2). In this context, the USAID policy of preferentially targeting the north and east is an important counterweight to the allocational decisions of the government.

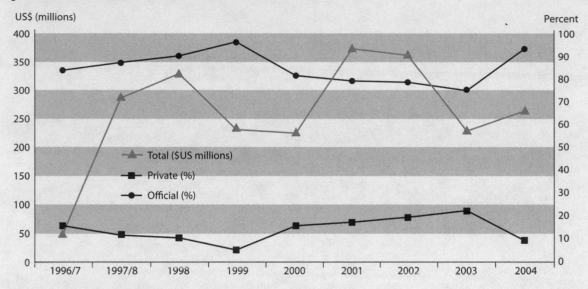

Figure 5. Total humanitarian assistance, private and official, 1996–2004

Source: UN-OCHA Financial Tracking Service, accessed 18 April 2005.
Note: Does not include China.

Definitions:
Official: Contributions to the Consolidated Appeal from governments, OPEC, and unearmarked funds from the UN, and donations by governments and UN agencies outside the appeal process; Private: Contributions to the Consolidated Appeal from "Private" sources and donations from NGOs and other non-official sources outside the appeal process.

Coordination Problems:
Aid in International Context

After 1995, it is impossible to discuss the nature of the North Korean food situation without reference to the humanitarian response, which consisted of three distinct components: aid channeled through multilateral institutions, and the WFP in particular; bilateral aid outside the WFP; and assistance from the NGO sector. The NGO sector has made important contributions to easing the crisis; several excellent studies have reviewed this experience in some detail (Smith 2002; Flake and Snyder 2003; Reed 2004). But the bulk of food assistance has passed through multilateral and bilateral channels, and this report focuses attention on them (Figure 5).

The United States has been the largest donor of food aid to North Korea, but it is certainly not the only one: European countries—both individually and through the European Commission—Japan, China, and South Korea have all provided aid as well (Figure 6). This multiplicity of donors necessarily created coordination problems among them. Since the monitoring of food aid is in effect a bargaining game between the international community and North Korea, handing more unconditional aid out can have adverse effects on the country's willingness to comply with basic humanitarian principles. Two countries, China and South Korea, provide concessional sales or grants of food to North Korea outside of the WFP. The nature of China's contracts with North Korea is not directly evident, but

Figure 6. Total food aid by major donors, 1996–2004

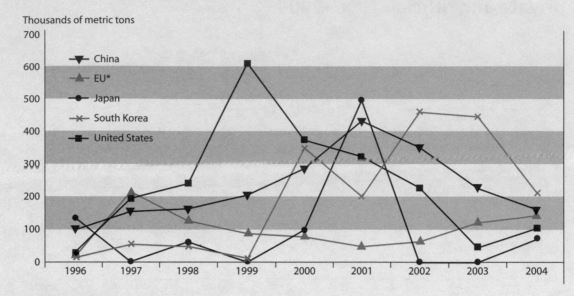

Thousands of metric tons

Legend:
- China
- EU*
- Japan
- South Korea
- United States

* EU includes contributions by the European Commission and EU member countries
Sources: Personal communication with INTERFAIS, June, 20, 2005.

there is no public evidence that they have conditioned aid either on overall policy reform or more particular principles of programmatic design, implementation, or monitoring. In the case of South Korea, aid has been provided with only the most minimal effort to monitor its distribution, as human rights groups in the country have noted.

There are numerous disadvantages in this arrangement. If China and South Korea become the suppliers of last resort, it provides the North Korean government the opportunity to further erode the modest and ineffective monitoring regime that is in place. North Korea has been able to avoid a more stringent monitoring regime—and has recently challenged the WFP's most basic mandate—as a result of alternative sources of less conditional supply.

In this respect, the policy choices of the South Korean government have been most disappointing. South Korea extended large-scale aid in the immediate aftermath of the floods in 1995, but was stung by North Korean efforts to hide the source of its assistance and pursued a restrictive aid policy until the inauguration of the Kim Dae Jung administration in 1998. Particularly after the historic summit meeting of 2000, both the Kim Dae Jung and Roh Moo Hyun administrations have extended large amounts of fertilizer and food aid to the North, in addition to other forms of transfers. Relatively open-ended aid commitments—totaling as much as half of North Korea's total food deficit according to the WFP—could have the unintended consequence of undercutting the WFP's attempts to uphold the norms embodied in international agreements to which South Korea is a party.

Policy Recommendations

During the 1990s, as many as one million North Koreans died in a famine that ranks as one of the most destructive of the 20th century. These deaths were largely unnecessary, the result of a misguided strategy of self-reliance that only served to increase the country's vulnerability. Slow to respond to the crisis—as closed, authoritarian governments so frequently are—the regime continued to criminalize many of the very coping strategies it had forced on its own population.

The humanitarian response was generous, with the international community providing $2 billion in food aid over the past decade. There can be little question that this aid served to relieve human suffering in North Korea. Yet nearly a decade after the famine crested, North Korea remains dependent on international largesse. Many of its citizens continue to face insecurity in their access to food, and the completely closed nature of the political system means they have few channels through which they can bring their grievances to light.

Nonetheless, the North Korean government continues to frustrate transparent, effective humanitarian relief. It can continue to pursue this strategy because the international community provides the country with aid despite these impediments. In effect, the North Korean government has used the suffering of its own people as a form of political leverage.

This study has implications for four sets of actors: the North Korean government itself; the donor community working through the WFP; the two countries—China and South Korea—who extend aid bilaterally; and the non-governmental organizations engaged in the country.

North Korea

The right to food is enshrined most clearly in the Universal Declaration of Human Rights and Article 11 of the International Covenant on Economic, Social and Cultural Rights (ICESCR), to which North Korea has been a party since December 1981.[4] The nature of governments' obligations under the ICESCR has subsequently been clarified through a wide-ranging consultative process, including most specifically by the Committee on Economic, Social and Cultural Rights in its General Comment No. 12 of 1999. The ICESCR does recognize that the right to adequate food can only be realized progressively, but General Comment 12 is clear that states have the obligation to "respect, protect, and fulfill" this right (para. 15).

The obligation to fulfill includes an obligation to provide, but recognizes implicitly that governments cannot necessarily meet this obligation on their own. The ICESCR and its subsequent interpretation therefore includes both an obligation to facilitate (General Comment 12, para. 15) and corresponding duties on the part of the international community to assist governments in distress or chronic need (ICESCR Article 11; General Comment 12, para. 36).

North Korea experienced severe economic shocks in the early 1990s, a tense standoff with respect to its nuclear weapons program, an uncertain political transition, and a succession of national disasters. Since October 2002, the country is once again involved in a dispute with the international community over its nuclear weapons ambitions. Each of these

---

[4]North Korea has also accepted related obligations as a signatory to the International Covenant on Civil and Political Rights (December 1981), the Convention on the Rights of the Child (October 1990), and the Convention on the Elimination of All Forms of Discrimination against Women (March 2001).

circumstances contributed to North Korea's economic isolation and posed severe policy challenges to the government.

None of these challenges, however absolve the government from its most basic of all responsibilities: to guarantee the survival needs of its people. To the contrary, national security arguments ring particularly hollow when authoritarian regimes use them to justify inhumane treatment of their populations. General Comment 12 (para. 6) is quite explicit on this point: "States have a core obligation to take the necessary action to mitigate and alleviate hunger as provided for in paragraph 2 of article 11, even in times of natural or other disasters."

The failure to provide is self-evident in the great famine of the mid-1990s and the ongoing evidence of food shortages. Equally, if not more disturbing, is the systematic evidence that the government did not adjust in a timely fashion to the shocks of the early 1990s and was slow in reaching out to humanitarian assistance as evidence of the famine became clear. Once the government did solicit external assistance, it not only engaged in a systematic effort to limit effective targeting, monitoring, and assessment of food delivery, but cut whole portions of the country off from desperately needed help. The result was a famine that killed as many as five percent of the populace—a substantial portion of them children—and consigned countless others to broken lives and stunted human development.

A key to resolving the North Korean hunger problem is the development of a functioning economy that generates sufficient foreign exchange earnings to purchase food on a commercial basis—just as its neighbors Japan, South Korea, and China do. While food security is an understandable national goal, it seldom, if ever, is best achieved through the pursuit of self-sufficiency. Given North Korea's basic endowments, it is highly unlikely that the country is capable of achieving food self-sufficiency; indeed, the famine and chronic food shortages have proven the point beyond dispute. Advocates of food security through self-sufficiency unwittingly play into misguided government aspirations in this regard and thus actually impede a solution to the ongoing crisis (Ahn 2005).

In reality, the only question is whether the necessary sources of external food supply continue to come from the international community or are financed by North Korea's own efforts. The precise contours of a reform program to achieve sustainable food imports must ultimately be decided by the government of North Korea. There is no one model, or blueprint, that North Korea must pursue, as the diversity of development experiences in the region attest.

However, the international community can assist. Many of North Korea's problems are long-term and developmental in nature. As the humanitarian community has long recognized, North Korea needs comprehensive technical assistance and development financing that can be provided in a relatively depoliticized way. Therefore North Korea's entry into the World Bank, International Monetary Fund (IMF) and Asian Development Bank, should be strongly supported even if membership in these institutions is only likely to occur with the resolution of the current nuclear standoff and the dispute over Japanese abductees.

In the meantime, North Korea will remain reliant on humanitarian relief. In this respect it is imperative that North Korea:

■ Lift the manifold restrictions and impediments that it continues to place on the humanitarian community and abide by the international agreements to which it is a signatory. While responsibility for North Korea's diplomatic problems are subject to dispute, these disputes do not absolve the government of its obligation to abide by the most basic and widely recognized principles governing humanitarian relief.

It is tempting to conclude that solving this most basic problem—achieving the ability to finance adequate food imports on a sustainable basis—is the only thing that needs to be done. But the economic reforms required to achieve this objective are only a necessary, not a sufficient, condition for improving access to food.

The North Korean food problem is not just a problem of production and capacity to import, but also an issue of distribution and entitlement; such questions necessarily depend on fundamental features of the political system. North Korea's tragedy could only have occurred in a system in which the political leadership was insulated from events on the ground, and shielded from political competition and freedom of association and speech.

- The improvement of human and civil rights, loosening controls on the press and allowing a genuine civil society to flourish would all enable the state to behave in a more responsive and responsible way toward its own citizens.

- Granting citizens secure property rights, and the freedom to trade and engage in private production without fear of retribution or confiscation would have a similar effect by increasing incomes and relieving pressures on the PDS.

While a better functioning economy is a prerequisite for solving the hunger problem, it alone will not permanently guarantee a North Korea free from hunger. Only political change can do that.

Participants in the World Food Program

Food crises trigger obligations not only on the part of the country experiencing them, but for the international community as well. The bulk of total aid provided to North Korea has come through the WFP, with the United States, the European Union, and Japan all playing significant roles at various times. A crucial first question is whether the international community should provide aid to North Korea at all. A variety of critics—not only in the United States but in Europe and South Korea as well—have argued that aid to North Korea only serves to prop up the current regime. Food insecurity is likely to remain a problem as long as this regime holds power. Some, therefore, conclude that the ultimate aim of the external community should be regime change in North Korea. Moreover, it has been suggested that the goal of policy reform would be advanced by coordinated action to cut North Korea off from the international economy and even from external supplies of food.

A reformist government would be desirable. But there are a number of flaws in jumping from this conclusion to prescriptions for how humanitarian assistance should be managed. First, the North Korean government has repeatedly shown its ability to impose extreme deprivation on its people. If the current regime was capable of surviving a devastating famine, it is highly dubious to assume that coordinated, wholesale reductions in food aid will necessarily lead to improved conditions or policy reform. In any case, there is little evidence that such coordination is possible given the competing political interests of the donor countries.

Moreover, this argument rests on a questionable utilitarian logic: that it is morally acceptable to sacrifice the innocent today in the uncertain prospect that lives will be saved or improved at some future point. This type of argument flies directly in the face of the fundamental rights that the international community is trying to uphold. While it is courageous for some to choose to make such a sacrifice for themselves, it is unacceptable for the outside community to choose it for the North Koreans. It is important to point out that those NGOs who did pull out of North Korea did so in the context of the WFP, bilateral donors, and other NGOs continuing to provide food and services. The calculus is very different when considering whether total food aid should be reduced or cut altogether.

It is also important to underscore that the humanitarian effort, however impeded, has almost certainly had positive effects on meeting the needs of vulnerable groups. Moreover, in the presence of functioning markets and diversion to undeserving groups or the market, food aid can still have beneficial effects for vulnerable populations by increasing overall supply and moderating prices. And markets are indeed developing: most local food production now finds it way onto the market, and the PDS exists largely as a mechanism for distributing foreign aid.

The sheer volume of aid that has been poured into the country and the apparent improvement in conditions since the peak famine years seem to suggest that aid has indeed had some beneficial effects through one or both of these channels. Yet the North Korean government has imposed severe restrictions on attempts to conduct rigorous analyses of nutritional status. Nutritional status remains at levels found only in the very poorest of countries. This does not mean that delivered aid is ineffective; it only demonstrates the uphill battle the humanitarian community must fight in a context where other features of the system make it difficult to be as effective as it otherwise could be. Just as the closed nature of the North Korean system inhibits effective program design, implementation, and monitoring, it prevents effective evaluation as well. There is much that remains hidden.

The arguments in favor of assistance seem clear, but one must simultaneously be clear-headed about the nature of the bargains that have been struck. It is likely that aid is not proffered in a non-discriminatory manner. Given the political stratification of North Korea and the inability of the WFP to achieve minimum standards of transparency and monitoring in its operations, deserving households—including politically disfavored households—are not getting the food intended for them or are being denied relief altogether. Recent refugee interviews confirm this point (Chang, forthcoming).

Furthermore, diversion is almost certainly occurring, and its scale is not small. If the off-the-record estimates of humanitarian assistance workers are to be believed, perhaps enough food to feed 3 to 10 percent of the North Korean populace is diverted. Some of this aid is almost surely consumed by the less deserving. The diversion that does go to the market is contributing to the creation of a privileged class of state-sector entrepreneurs and their allies. North Korea is becoming an increasingly stratified society, with a sharp division between those with access to foreign exchange and food and those without.

The administrators of the international aid program have worked in extremely difficult circumstances, even heroically, to assist the people of North Korea. Yet it is critical that within these constraints, the WFP continue to be not only the humanitarian face of the international community but a voice of conscience for those deprived of the most fundamental right to food. The WFP and its associated donors must:

- Continue to highlight government practices that impede the delivery of food to vulnerable groups;

- Continue to uphold the humanitarian principles outlined above;

- Continue to abide by the principle that aid will not be extended to counties where access is denied;

- Explore technical solutions to improve the quality of monitoring, such as the introduction of modern inventory-management systems that can reduce the scope for diversion and assure donors that their contributions were used as intended.

In the end, however, regardless of technical improvements of the aid program, the international community must make a concerted and coordinated effort to wean North Korea from humanitarian assistance. This would involve outlining and negotiating a path of reduced humanitarian assistance over time, subject to reversal in the face of natural disasters. One of the most disturbing findings is the evidence that North Korea seems unwilling to purchase grain. This practice cannot continue. The burden of financing North Korea's food deficit should be shifted from the international humanitarian community—which is facing pressing needs elsewhere—onto the North Koreans themselves.

Resources are not limitless, and there are other competing needs around the world. In the absence of significant changes in North Korean government policy, scarce resources may be better deployed elsewhere.

Bilateral Donors Outside of the WFP: China and South Korea

Two countries, China and South Korea, provide concessional sales or grants of food to North Korea outside of the WFP. It is not evident that China has conditioned aid either on overall policy reform or more particular principles of programmatic design, implementation, or monitoring. In the case of South Korea, concessional food assistance has been provided without any attempt to assess conditions or target vulnerable groups, and with only perfunctory attempts to monitor its distribution.

In this regard the practices of the South Korean government have been most disappointing. Large, relatively open-ended aid commitments—amounting to nearly 90 percent of total WFP appeals—are having the unintended consequence of undermining the WFP's attempts to uphold the norms embodied in international agreements to which South Korea is a party. Special circumstances bind the South and North Korean people together. However, if China and South Korea assume the role of suppliers of last resort, North Korea will be able to avoid greater accountability.

- China and South Korea should channel future concessional food assistance through the WFP. Their experience and voice would be of invaluable assistance to WFP operations—both generally and in North Korea—and would facilitate the coordinated approach needed to reduce North Korea's dependence on humanitarian assistance.

NGOs

Given that most food aid passes through official channels, the outstanding and innovative work that has been done by the variety of NGOs who have worked in North Korea must be addressed. A handful of influential organizations have taken the decision to leave, while others have stayed in the hope of continuing to do effective work.

These organizations are private, and it is ultimately up to them how they choose to organize relations with the North Korean government. A number of them have adopted innovative strategies that manage to provide assistance while also serving to advance the cause of basic human rights and the empowerment of the people whom they serve.

■ At the same time, within their limited freedom of maneuver, it is hoped that NGOs focus not only on their humanitarian mission, but on the basic rights that are a necessary condition to ensure that entitlements to food are guaranteed.

The failure of the North Korean government to guarantee adequate supplies of food to its population is related directly to the government's denial of a battery of other rights to its citizens: to confront public officials with their shortcomings, to publicize information that allows government officials to know the extent of distress, and to organize collectively in the face of injustice and deprivation. In the presence of these rights, North Korea might well have experienced food shortages, but neither the great famine nor the chronic shortages of food would have been possible. NGOs working in North Korea would not be toiling in an unsupportive environment or struggling with the consequences of an ongoing food emergency. Their scarce human and financial resources could have been deployed to other areas of need where local governments would be more supportive of their mission. Therein lies the link between access to food and human rights.

References

Ahn, Christine. 2005. *Policy Brief No. 11: Famine and the Future of Food Security in North Korea*. Oakland CA: Food First/Institute for Food and Development Policy.

Bennett, John. 1999. "North Korea: The Politics of Food Aid." *RRN Network Paper* 28. London: Overseas Development Institute, p. 16.

Brooke, James. "North Korea, Facing Food Shortages, Mobilizes Millions From the Cities to Help Rice Farmers." *New York Times*. June 1, 2005, Late Edition: Section A, Page 8, Column 1.

Chang, Christine. Research on North Korean refugees in China conducted for the U.S. Committee for Human Rights in North Korea (forthcoming).

Dammers, Chris, et al. 2005. Report for the Evaluation of ECHO's Actions in the Democratic People's Republic of Korea 2001 - 2004. United Kingdom: Agua Consulting.

Flake, L. Gordon, and Scott Snyder. 2003. *Paved With Good Intentions: The NGO Experience in North Korea*. Westport: Praeger.

Food and Agricultural Organization (FAO), Special Advisors to the Director – General. 1998. "Rome Declaration on World Food Security and World Food Summit Plan of Action." Rome: Food and Agricultural Organization of the United Nations. www.fao.org/documents/show_cdr.asp?url_file=/docrep/003/w3613e/w3613e00.htm

Food and Agricultural Organization (FAO). 2004. *The State of Food Insecurity in the World 2004*. Rome: Food and Agricultural Organization.

Food and Agricultural Organization and World Food Programme (FAO/WFP). December 22, 1995. "Special Report - FAO/WFP Crop and Food Supply Assessment Mission to the Democratic People's Republic of Korea." (accessed April 27, 2005). http://www.fao.org/documents/show_cdr.asp?url_file=/DOCREP/004/W0051E/W0051E00.htm

Food and Agricultural Organization and World Food Programme (FAO/WFP). December 6, 1996. "Special Report- FAO/WFP Crop and Food Supply Assessment Mission to the Democratic People's Republic of Korea." (accessed April 27, 2005). http://www.fao.org/documents/show_cdr.asp?url_file=/DOCREP/004/W3690E/W3690E00.htm

Food and Agricultural Organization and World Food Programme (FAO/WFP). November 25, 1997. "Special Report- FAO/WFP Crop and Food Supply Assessment Mission to the Democratic People's Republic of Korea." (accessed April 27, 2005). http://www.fao.org/documents/show_cdr.asp?url_file=/DOCREP/004/W7289E/W7289E00.htm

Food and Agricultural Organization and World Food Programme (FAO/WFP). June 25, 1998. "Special Report- FAO/WFP Crop and Food Supply Assessment Mission to the Democratic People's Republic of Korea." (accessed April 27, 2005). http://www.fao.org/documents/show_cdr.asp?url_file=/DOCREP/004/W9066E/W9066E00.htm

Food and Agricultural Organization and World Food Programme (FAO/WFP). November 12, 1998. "Special Report- FAO/WFP Crop and Food Supply Assessment Mission to the Democratic People's Republic of Korea." (accessed April 27, 2005). http://www.fao.org/documents/show_cdr.asp?url_file=/DOCREP/004/X0449E/X0449E00.HTM

Food and Agricultural Organization and World Food Programme (FAO/WFP). June 29, 1999. "Special Report - FAO/WFP Crop and Food Supply Assessment Mission to the Democratic People's Republic of Korea." (accessed April 27, 2005). http://www.fao.org/documents/show_cdr.asp?url_file=/docrep/004/x2437e/x2437e00.htm

Food and Agricultural Organization and World Food Programme (FAO/WFP). November 8, 1999. "Special Report - FAO/WFP Crop and Food Supply Assessment Mission to the Democratic People's Republic of Korea." (accessed April 27, 2005). http://www.fao.org/documents/show_cdr.asp?url_file=/docrep/004/x3691e/x3691e00.htm

Food and Agricultural Organization and World Food Programme (FAO/WFP). October 30, 2003. "Special Report- FAO/WFP Crop and Food Supply Assessment Mission to the Democratic People's Republic of Korea." (accessed April 27, 2005). http://www.fao.org/documents/show_cdr.asp?url_file=/DOCREP/006/J0741E/J0741E00.htm

Food and Agricultural Organization and World Food Programme (FAO/WFP). November 22, 2004. "Special Report- FAO/WFP Crop and Food Supply Assessment Mission to the Democratic People's Republic of Korea." (accessed April 27, 2005). http://www.fao.org/documents/show_cdr.asp?url_file=/docrep/007/j2972e/j2972e00.htm

Food and Agricultural Organization Statistical Databases (FAOSTAT). Database. Geneva: Food and Agricultural Organization of the United Nations. (accessed April 27, 2005). http://faostat.fao.org/

Good Friends Center for Peace, Human Rights and Refugees. 2000. "Understanding the Responses of the North Koreans to the Social and Economic Condition of North Korea." Seoul.

Good Friends Center for Peace, Human Rights and Refugees. March, 2004. "Human Rights in North Korea and the Food Crisis." Seoul.

Good Friends Center for Peace, Human Rights and Refugees. January, 2005. "North Korea Today." Seoul.

Goodkind, Daniel, and Lorraine West. 2001. "The North Korean Famine and Its Demographic Impact." *Population and Development Review* 27, no. 2: 219-38.

Hawk, David. 2003. *The Hidden Gulag.* Washington: U.S. Committee for Human Rights in North Korea.

International Food Aid Information System (INTERFAIS). 2004. "Food Aid Monitor, 2004 Food Aid Flows." World Food Programme. http://www.wfp.org/interfais

Kim, Woon-keun, Lee Hyun-ok, and Daniel A. Sumner. 1998. "Assessing the Food Situation in North Korea." *Economic Development and Cultural Change.* 46:3 519-34.

Korea Development Institute (KDI). 1999. *Nutritional Problems of North Korean Children.* Seoul. Lee, Suk. 2003. *Food Shortages and Economic Institutions in the Democratic People's Republic of Korea.* Unpublished doctoral dissertation, Department of Economics, University of Warwick, Coventry, UK.

Nam, Sung Wook. 2004. "Food Security in North Korea and Its Economic Outlook." Department of North Korean Study, Korea University, Seoul, South Korea.

Natsios, Andrew S. 2001. *The Great North Korean Famine.* Washington: U.S. Institute for Peace.

Noland, Marcus. 2000. *Avoiding the Apocalypse: The Future of the Two Koreas.* Washington: Institute for International Economics.

Noland, Marcus. 2004. "Famine and Reform in North Korea." *Asian Economic Papers.* 3:2 1-40.

Noland, Marcus, Sherman Robinson, and Tao Wang. 2001. "Famine in North Korea: Causes and Cures." *Economic Development and Cultural Change* 49, no. 4.

Reed, P. Edward. "Unlikely Partners: Humanitarian Aid Agencies and North Korea." *A New International Engagement Framework for North Korea.* Ed. Ahn Choong-yong, Nicholas Eberstadt, and Lee Young-sun. Washington: Korea Economic Institute of America, 2004. pp. 199 – 229.

Robinson, W. Courtland, et al. Compilation of interviews of 1,019 North Korean Refugees. June 1998. Seoul: Korean Buddhist Sharing Movement (KBSM).

Robinson, W. Courtland, Myung Ken Lee, Kenneth Hill, and Gilbert Burnham. 1999. "Mortality in North Korean Migrant Households: A Retrospective Study." *Lancet* 354 (July-December): 291-295.

Robinson, W. Courtland, Myung Ken Lee, Kenneth Hill, and Gilbert Burnham. 2001. "Demographic Methods to Assess Food Insecurity." *Prehospital and Disaster Medicine* 16, 4 (October-December): 286-292.

Smith, Hazel. July 2002. "Overcoming Humanitarian Dilemmas in the DPRK (North Korea)." *United States Institute for Peace Special Report 90.* Washington: US Institute for Peace.

Smith, Heather. 1998. "The Food Economy: The Catalyst for Collapse?" in Marcus Noland (ed.). *Economic Integration on the Korean Peninsula.* Washington: Institute for International Economics.

Sphere Project. 2004. Humanitarian Charter and Minimum Standards in Disaster Response. Geneva.

Woo-Cumings, Meredith. 2002. "The Political Ecology of Famine: The North Korean Catastrophe and Its Lessons." *ADB Institute Research Paper* 31. Tokyo: Asian Development Bank Institute.

World Food Programme. November 1998. "Nutritional Survey of the DPRK." Geneva.

World Food Programme. April 2002. *The WFP DPR Korea Monthly Update* No. 39. Pyongyang.

World Food Programme. May 2002. *The WFP DPR Korea Monthly Update* No. 40. Pyongyang.

World Food Programme. November 2002. *The WFP DPR Korea Monthly Update* No. 46. Pyongyang.

World Food Programme. January 2003. *The WFP DPR Korea Monthly Update* No. 60. Pyongyang.

World Food Programme. February 20, 2003. "Child Nutrition Survey Shows Improvements in DPRK But UN Agencies Concerned About Holding Onto Gains." Pyongyang/ Geneva.

World Food Programme. May 21, 2003. "Public Distribution System (PDS) in DPRK." DPR Korea Country Office.

World Food Programme. January 2004. *The WFP DPR Korea Monthly Update* No. 60. Pyongyang.

World Food Programme. January 31, 2005. *The WFP DPR Korea Monthly Update*. Pyongyang.

World Food Programme International Food Aid Information System (INTERFAIS). May 2004. "Food Aid Flows 2003." Geneva. (accessed April 27, 2005). http://www.wfp. org/interfais/

United Nations Division for the Advancement of Women. Department of Economic and Social Affairs. 1981. "Convention on the Elimination of All Forms of Discrimination Against Women." http://www.un.org/womenwatch/daw/cedaw/cedaw.htm

United Nations General Assembly. 1948. "Universal Declaration of Human Rights." http:// www.un.org/Overview/rights.html

United Nations General Assembly. 1966. "International Covenant on Civil and Political Rights." http://www.unhchr.ch/html/menu3/b/a_ccpr.htm

United Nations General Assembly. 1966. "International Covenant on Economic, Social, and Cultural Rights." http://www.unhchr.ch/html/menu3/b/a_cescr.htm

United Nations General Assembly. 1989. "The Convention on the Rights of the Child." http://www.unicef.org/crc/crc.htm

United States Department of Agriculture Foreign Agricultural Service (USDA). 2002. http://www.fas.usda/gov/pecad2/highlights/2002/06/nkorea/index.htm

Ziegler, Jean. 2002. "Economic, Social, and Cultural Rights: the Right to Food," Report by the Special Rapporteur on the Right to Food. Commision on Human Rights, fifty-eighth session, E/CN.4/2002/58, United Nations Economic and Social Council.

Office of the High Commissioner of Human Rights
International Covenant on Economic, Social and Cultural Rights

Adopted and opened for signature, ratification and accession by General Assembly resolution 2200A (XXI) of 16 December 1966

entry into force **3 January 1976, in accordance with article 27**

Preamble

The States Parties to the present Covenant,

Considering that, in accordance with the principles proclaimed in the Charter of the United Nations, recognition of the inherent dignity and of the equal and inalienable rights of all members of the human family is the foundation of freedom, justice and peace in the world,

Recognizing that these rights derive from the inherent dignity of the human person,

Recognizing that, in accordance with the Universal Declaration of Human Rights, the ideal of free human beings enjoying freedom from fear and want can only be achieved if conditions are created whereby everyone may enjoy his economic, social and cultural rights, as well as his civil and political rights,

Considering the obligation of States under the Charter of the United Nations to promote universal respect for, and observance of, human rights and freedoms,

Realizing that the individual, having duties to other individuals and to the community to which he belongs, is under a responsibility to strive for the promotion and observance of the rights recognized in the present Covenant,

Agree upon the following articles.

PART I

Article 1

1. All peoples have the right of self-determination. By virtue of that right they freely determine their political status and freely pursue their economic, social and cultural development.

2. All peoples may, for their own ends, freely dispose of their natural wealth and resources without prejudice to any obligations arising out of international economic co-operation, based upon the principle of mutual benefit, and international law. In no case may a people be deprived of its own means of subsistence.

3. The States Parties to the present Covenant, including those having responsibility for the administration of Non-Self-Governing and Trust Territories, shall promote the realization of the right of self-determination, and shall respect that right, in conformity with the provisions of the Charter of the United Nations.

PART II

Article 2

1. Each State Party to the present Covenant undertakes to take steps, individually and through international assistance and co-operation, especially economic and technical, to the maximum of its available resources, with a view to achieving progressively the full realization of the rights recognized in the present Covenant by all appropriate means, including particularly the adoption of legislative measures. General comment on its implementation

2. The States Parties to the present Covenant undertake to guarantee that the rights enunciated in the present Covenant will be exercised without discrimination of any kind as to race, colour, sex, language, religion, political or other opinion, national or social origin, property, birth or other status.

3. Developing countries, with due regard to human rights and their national economy, may determine to what extent they would guarantee the economic rights recognized in the present Covenant to non-nationals.

Article 3
The States Parties to the present Covenant undertake to ensure the equal right of men and women to the enjoyment of all economic, social and cultural rights set forth in the present Covenant.

Article 4
The States Parties to the present Covenant recognize that, in the enjoyment of those rights provided by the State in conformity with the present Covenant, the State may subject such rights only to such limitations as are determined by law only in so far as this may be compatible with the nature of these rights and solely for the purpose of promoting the general welfare in a democratic society.

Article 5
1. Nothing in the present Covenant may be interpreted as implying for any State, group or person any right to engage in any activity or to perform any act aimed at the destruction of any of the rights or freedoms recognized herein, or at their limitation to a greater extent than is provided for in the present Covenant.

2. No restriction upon or derogation from any of the fundamental human rights recognized or existing in any country in virtue of law, conventions, regulations or custom shall be admitted on the pretext that the present Covenant does not recognize such rights or that it recognizes them to a lesser extent.

PART III

Article 6
1. The States Parties to the present Covenant recognize the right to work, which includes the right of everyone to the opportunity to gain his living by work which he freely chooses or accepts, and will take appropriate steps to safeguard this right.

2. The steps to be taken by a State Party to the present Covenant to achieve the full realization of this right shall include technical and vocational guidance and training programmes, policies and techniques to achieve steady economic, social and cultural development and full and productive employment under conditions safeguarding fundamental political and economic freedoms to the individual.

Article 7
The States Parties to the present Covenant recognize the right of everyone to the enjoyment of just and favourable conditions of work which ensure, in particular:
>   (a) Remuneration which provides all workers, as a minimum, with:
>   (i) Fair wages and equal remuneration for work of equal value without distinction of any kind, in particular women being guaranteed conditions of work not inferior to those enjoyed by men, with equal pay for equal work;
>   (ii) A decent living for themselves and their families in accordance with the provisions of the present Covenant;
>   (b) Safe and healthy working conditions;
>   (c) Equal opportunity for everyone to be promoted in his employment to an appropriate higher level, subject to no considerations other than those of seniority and competence;
>   (d) Rest, leisure and reasonable limitation of working hours and periodic holidays with pay, as well as remuneration for public holidays

Article 8

1. The States Parties to the present Covenant undertake to ensure:

(a) The right of everyone to form trade unions and join the trade union of his choice, subject only to the rules of the organization concerned, for the promotion and protection of his economic and social interests. No restrictions may be placed on the exercise of this right other than those prescribed by law and which are necessary in a democratic society in the interests of national security or public order or for the protection of the rights and freedoms of others;

(b) The right of trade unions to establish national federations or confederations and the right of the latter to form or join international trade-union organizations;

(c) The right of trade unions to function freely subject to no limitations other than those prescribed by law and which are necessary in a democratic society in the interests of national security or public order or for the protection of the rights and freedoms of others;

(d) The right to strike, provided that it is exercised in conformity with the laws of the particular country.

2. This article shall not prevent the imposition of lawful restrictions on the exercise of these rights by members of the armed forces or of the police or of the administration of the State.

3. Nothing in this article shall authorize States Parties to the International Labour Organisation Convention of 1948 concerning Freedom of Association and Protection of the Right to Organize to take legislative measures which would prejudice, or apply the law in such a manner as would prejudice, the guarantees provided for in that Convention.

Article 9

The States Parties to the present Covenant recognize the right of everyone to social security, including social insurance.

Article 10

The States Parties to the present Covenant recognize that:

1. The widest possible protection and assistance should be accorded to the family, which is the natural and fundamental group unit of society, particularly for its establishment and while it is responsible for the care and education of dependent children. Marriage must be entered into with the free consent of the intending spouses.

2. Special protection should be accorded to mothers during a reasonable period before and after childbirth. During such period working mothers should be accorded paid leave or leave with adequate social security benefits.

3. Special measures of protection and assistance should be taken on behalf of all children and young persons without any discrimination for reasons of parentage or other conditions. Children and young persons should be protected from economic and social exploitation. Their employment in work harmful to their morals or health or dangerous to life or likely to hamper their normal development should be punishable by law. States should also set age limits below which the paid employment of child labour should be prohibited and punishable by law.

Article 11

1. The States Parties to the present Covenant recognize the right of everyone to an adequate standard of living for himself and his family, including adequate food, clothing and housing, and to the continuous improvement of living conditions. The States Parties will take appropriate steps to ensure the realization of this right, recognizing to this effect the essential importance of international co-operation based on free consent.

2. The States Parties to the present Covenant, recognizing the fundamental right of everyone to be free from hunger, shall take, individually and through international co-operation, the measures, including specific programmes, which are needed:

(a) To improve methods of production, conservation and distribution of food by making full use of technical and scientific knowledge, by disseminating knowledge of the principles of nutrition and by developing or reforming agrarian systems in such a way as to achieve the most efficient development and utilization of natural resources;

(b) Taking into account the problems of both food-importing and food-exporting countries, to ensure an equitable distribution of world food supplies in relation to need.

Article 12

1. The States Parties to the present Covenant recognize the right of everyone to the enjoyment of the highest attainable standard of physical and mental health.

2. The steps to be taken by the States Parties to the present Covenant to achieve the full realization of this right shall include those necessary for:

(a) The provision for the reduction of the stillbirth-rate and of infant mortality and for the healthy development of the child;
(b) The improvement of all aspects of environmental and industrial hygiene;
(c) The prevention, treatment and control of epidemic, endemic, occupational and other diseases;
(d) The creation of conditions which would assure to all medical service and medical attention in the event of sickness.

Article 13

1. The States Parties to the present Covenant recognize the right of everyone to education. They agree that education shall be directed to the full development of the human personality and the sense of its dignity, and shall strengthen the respect for human rights and fundamental freedoms. They further agree that education shall enable all persons to participate effectively in a free society, promote understanding, tolerance and friendship among all nations and all racial, ethnic or religious groups, and further the activities of the United Nations for the maintenance of peace.

2. The States Parties to the present Covenant recognize that, with a view to achieving the full realization of this right:
(a) Primary education shall be compulsory and available free to all;
(b) Secondary education in its different forms, including technical and vocational secondary education, shall be made generally available and accessible to all by every appropriate means, and in particular by the progressive introduction of free education;
(c) Higher education shall be made equally accessible to all, on the basis of capacity, by every appropriate means, and in particular by the progressive introduction of free education;
(d) Fundamental education shall be encouraged or intensified as far as possible for those persons who have not received or completed the whole period of their primary education;
(e) The development of a system of schools at all levels shall be actively pursued, an adequate fellowship system shall be established, and the material conditions of teaching staff shall be continuously improved.

3. The States Parties to the present Covenant undertake to have respect for the liberty of parents and, when applicable, legal guardians to choose for their children schools, other than those established by the public authorities, which conform to such minimum educational standards as may be laid down or approved by the State and to ensure the religious and moral education of their children in conformity with their own convictions.

4. No part of this article shall be construed so as to interfere with the liberty of individuals and bodies to establish and direct educational institutions, subject always to the observance of the principles set forth in paragraph I of this article and to the requirement that the education given in such institutions shall conform to such minimum standards as may be laid down by the State.

Article 14

Each State Party to the present Covenant which, at the time of becoming a Party, has not been able to secure in its metropolitan territory or other territories under its jurisdiction compulsory primary education, free of charge, undertakes, within two years, to work out and adopt a detailed plan of action for the progressive implementation, within a reasonable number of years, to be fixed in the plan, of the principle of compulsory education free of charge for all.

Article 15

1. The States Parties to the present Covenant recognize the right of everyone:
   > (a) To take part in cultural life;
   > (b) To enjoy the benefits of scientific progress and its applications;
   > (c) To benefit from the protection of the moral and material interests resulting from any scientific, literary or artistic production of which he is the author.

2. The steps to be taken by the States Parties to the present Covenant to achieve the full realization of this right shall include those necessary for the conservation, the development and the diffusion of science and culture.

3. The States Parties to the present Covenant undertake to respect the freedom indispensable for scientific research and creative activity.

4. The States Parties to the present Covenant recognize the benefits to be derived from the encouragement and development of international contacts and co-operation in the scientific and cultural fields.

PART IV

Article 16

1. The States Parties to the present Covenant undertake to submit in conformity with this part of the Covenant reports on the measures which they have adopted and the progress made in achieving the observance of the rights recognized herein.

2. (a) All reports shall be submitted to the Secretary-General of the United Nations, who shall transmit copies to the Economic and Social Council for consideration in accordance with the provisions of the present Covenant;
   > (b) The Secretary-General of the United Nations shall also transmit to the specialized agencies copies of the reports, or any relevant parts therefrom, from States Parties to the present Covenant which are also members of these specialized agencies in so far as these reports, or parts therefrom, relate to any matters which fall within the responsibilities of the said agencies in accordance with their constitutional instruments.

Article 17

1. The States Parties to the present Covenant shall furnish their reports in stages, in accordance with a programme to be established by the Economic and Social Council within one year of the entry into force of the present Covenant after consultation with the States Parties and the specialized agencies concerned.

2. Reports may indicate factors and difficulties affecting the degree of fulfilment of obligations under the present Covenant.

3. Where relevant information has previously been furnished to the United Nations or to any specialized agency by any State Party to the present Covenant, it will not be necessary to reproduce that information, but a precise reference to the information so furnished will suffice.

Article 18

Pursuant to its responsibilities under the Charter of the United Nations in the field of human rights and fundamental freedoms, the Economic and Social Council may make arrangements with the specialized agencies in respect of their reporting to it on the progress made in achieving the observance of the provisions of the present Covenant falling within the scope of their activities. These reports may include particulars of decisions and recommendations on such implementation adopted by their competent organs.

Article 19

The Economic and Social Council may transmit to the Commission on Human Rights for study and general recommendation or, as appropriate, for information the reports concerning human rights submitted by States in accordance with articles 16 and 17, and those concerning human rights submitted by the specialized agencies in accordance with article 18.

Article 20

The States Parties to the present Covenant and the specialized agencies concerned may submit comments to the Economic and Social Council on any general recommendation under article 19 or reference to such general recommendation in any report of the Commission on Human Rights or any documentation referred to therein.

Article 21

The Economic and Social Council may submit from time to time to the General Assembly reports with recommendations of a general nature and a summary of the information received from the States Parties to the present Covenant and the specialized agencies on the measures taken and the progress made in achieving general observance of the rights recognized in the present Covenant.

Article 22

The Economic and Social Council may bring to the attention of other organs of the United Nations, their subsidiary organs and specialized agencies concerned with furnishing technical assistance any matters arising out of the reports referred to in this part of the present Covenant which may assist such bodies in deciding, each within its field of competence, on the advisability of international measures likely to contribute to the effective progressive implementation of the present Covenant.

Article 23

The States Parties to the present Covenant agree that international action for the achievement of the rights recognized in the present Covenant includes such methods as the conclusion of conventions, the adoption of recommendations, the furnishing of technical assistance and the holding of regional meetings and technical meetings for the purpose of consultation and study organized in conjunction with the Governments concerned.

Article 24

Nothing in the present Covenant shall be interpreted as impairing the provisions of the Charter of the United Nations and of the constitutions of the specialized agencies which define the respective responsibilities of the various organs of the United Nations and of the specialized agencies in regard to the matters dealt with in the present Covenant.

Article 25

Nothing in the present Covenant shall be interpreted as impairing the inherent right of all peoples to enjoy and utilize fully and freely their natural wealth and resources.

PART V

Article 26

1. The present Covenant is open for signature by any State Member of the United Nations or member of any of its specialized agencies, by any State Party to the Statute of the International Court of Justice, and by any other State which has been invited by the General Assembly of the United Nations to become a party to the present Covenant.

2. The present Covenant is subject to ratification. Instruments of ratification shall be deposited with the Secretary-General of the United Nations.

3. The present Covenant shall be open to accession by any State referred to in paragraph 1 of this article.

4. Accession shall be effected by the deposit of an instrument of accession with the Secretary-General of the United Nations.

5. The Secretary-General of the United Nations shall inform all States which have signed the present Covenant or acceded to it of the deposit of each instrument of ratification or accession.

Article 27

1. The present Covenant shall enter into force three months after the date of the deposit with the Secretary-General of the United Nations of the thirty-fifth instrument of ratification or instrument of accession.

2. For each State ratifying the present Covenant or acceding to it after the deposit of the thirty-fifth instrument of ratification or instrument of accession, the present Covenant shall enter into force three months after the date of the deposit of its own instrument of ratification or instrument of accession.

Article 28

The provisions of the present Covenant shall extend to all parts of federal States without any limitations or exceptions.

Article 29

1. Any State Party to the present Covenant may propose an amendment and file it with the Secretary-General of the United Nations. The Secretary-General shall thereupon communicate any proposed amendments to the States Parties to the present Covenant with a request that they notify him whether they favour a conference of States Parties for the purpose of considering and voting upon the proposals. In the event that at least one third of the States Parties favours such a conference, the Secretary-General shall convene the conference under the auspices of the United Nations. Any amendment adopted by a majority of the States Parties present and voting at the conference shall be submitted to the General Assembly of the United Nations for approval.

2. Amendments shall come into force when they have been approved by the General Assembly of the United Nations and accepted by a two-thirds majority of the States Parties to the present Covenant in accordance with their respective constitutional processes.

3. When amendments come into force they shall be binding on those States Parties which have accepted them, other States Parties still being bound by the provisions of the present Covenant and any earlier amendment which they have accepted.

Article 30

Irrespective of the notifications made under article 26, paragraph 5, the Secretary-General of the United Nations shall inform all States referred to in paragraph I of the same article of the following particulars:
    (a) Signatures, ratifications and accessions under article 26;
    (b) The date of the entry into force of the present Covenant under article 27 and the date of the entry into force of any amendments under article 29.

Article 31

1. The present Covenant, of which the Chinese, English, French, Russian and Spanish texts are equally authentic, shall be deposited in the archives of the United Nations.

2. The Secretary-General of the United Nations shall transmit certified copies of the present Covenant to all States referred to in article 26.

Appendix B

UNITED NATIONS

E

Economic and Social Council

Distr.
GENERAL
E/C.12/1999/5
12 May 1999
Original: ENGLISH

---

*The right to adequate food (Art.11) : . 12/05/99.
E/C.12/1999/5. (General Comments)*

Convention Abbreviation: CESCR
COMMITTEE ON ECONOMIC, SOCIAL
AND CULTURAL RIGHTS
Twentieth session
Geneva, 26 April-14 May 1999
Agenda item 7

SUBSTANTIVE ISSUES ARISING IN THE IMPLEMENTATION OF THE
INTERNATIONAL COVENANT ON ECONOMIC, SOCIAL
AND CULTURAL RIGHTS:

GENERAL COMMENT 12

The right to adequate food

(Art. 11)

(Twentieth session, 1999) *

Introduction and basic premises

1. The human right to adequate food is recognized in several instruments under international law. The International Covenant on Economic, Social and Cultural Rights deals more comprehensively than any other instrument with this right. Pursuant to article 11.1 of the Covenant, States parties recognize "the right of everyone to an adequate standard of living for himself and his family, including adequate food, clothing and housing, and to the continuous improvement of living conditions", while pursuant to article 11.2 they recognize that more immediate and urgent steps may be needed to ensure "the fundamental right to freedom from hunger and malnutrition". The human right to adequate food is of crucial importance for the enjoyment of all rights. It applies to everyone; thus the reference in Article 11.1 to "himself and his family" does not imply any limitation upon the applicability of this right to individuals or to female-headed households.

2. The Committee has accumulated significant information pertaining to the right to adequate food through examination of State parties' reports over the years since 1979. The Committee has noted that while reporting guidelines are available relating to the right to adequate food, only few States parties have provided information sufficient and precise enough to enable the Committee to determine the prevailing situation in the countries concerned with respect to this right and to identify the obstacles to

---

* Contained in document E/C.12/1999/5.

its realization. This General Comment aims to identify some of the principal issues which the Committee considers to be important in relation to the right to adequate food. Its preparation was triggered by the request of Member States during the 1996 World Food Summit, for a better definition of the rights relating to food in article 11 of the Covenant, and by a special request to the Committee to give particular attention to the Summit Plan of Action in monitoring the implementation of the specific measures provided for in article 11 of the Covenant.

3. In response to these requests, the Committee reviewed the relevant reports and documentation of the Commission on Human Rights and of the Sub-Commission on Prevention of Discrimination and Protection of Minorities on the right to adequate food as a human right; devoted a day of general discussion to this issue at its seventeenth session in 1997, taking into consideration the draft international code of conduct on the human right to adequate food prepared by international non-governmental organizations; participated in two expert consultations on the right to adequate food as a human right organized by the Office of the United Nations High Commissioner for Human Rights (OHCHR), in Geneva in December 1997, and in Rome in November 1998 co-hosted by the Food and Agriculture Organization of the United Nations (FAO), and noted their final reports. In April 1999 the Committee participated in a symposium on "The substance and politics of a human rights approach to food and nutrition policies and programmes", organized by the Administrative Committee on Co-ordination/Sub-Committee on Nutrition of the United Nations at its twenty-sixth session in Geneva and hosted by OHCHR.

4. The Committee affirms that the right to adequate food is indivisibly linked to the inherent dignity of the human person and is indispensable for the fulfilment of other human rights enshrined in the International Bill of Human Rights. It is also inseparable from social justice, requiring the adoption of appropriate economic, environmental and social policies, at both the national and international levels, oriented to the eradication of poverty and the fulfilment of all human rights for all.

5. Despite the fact that the international community has frequently reaffirmed the importance of full respect for the right to adequate food, a disturbing gap still exists between the standards set in article 11 of the Covenant and the situation prevailing in many parts of the world. More than 840 million people throughout the world, most of them in developing countries, are chronically hungry; millions of people are suffering from famine as the result of natural disasters, the increasing incidence of civil strife and wars in some regions and the use of food as a political weapon. The Committee observes that while the problems of hunger and malnutrition are often particularly acute in developing countries, malnutrition, under-nutrition and other problems which relate to the right to adequate food and the right to freedom from hunger, also exist in some of the most economically developed countries. Fundamentally, the roots of the problem of hunger and malnutrition are not lack of food but lack of *access* to available food, inter alia because of poverty, by large segments of the world's population

Normative content of article 11, paragraphs 1 and 2

6. The right to adequate food is realized when every man, woman and child, alone or in community with others, has physical and economic access at all times to adequate food or means for its procurement. The *right to adequate food* shall therefore not be interpreted in a narrow or restrictive sense which equates it with a minimum package of calories, proteins and other specific nutrients. The *right to adequate food* will have to be realized progressively. However, States have a core obligation to take the necessary action to mitigate and alleviate hunger as provided for in paragraph 2 of article 11, even in times of natural or other disasters.

Adequacy and sustainability of food availability and access

7. The concept of *adequacy* is particularly significant in relation to the right to food since it serves to underline a number of factors which must be taken into account in determining whether particular foods or diets that are accessible can be considered the most appropriate under given circumstances for the

---

[1]/ Originally three levels of obligations were proposed: to respect, protect and assist/fulfil. (See Right to adequate food as a human right, Study Series No. 1, New York, 1989 (United Nations publication, Sales No. E.89.XIV.2).) The intermediate level of "to facilitate" has been proposed as a Committee category, but the Committee decided to maintain the three levels of obligation.

purposes of article 11 of the Covenant. The notion of *sustainability* is intrinsically linked to the notion of adequate food or food *security*, implying food being accessible for both present and future generations. The precise meaning of "adequacy" is to a large extent determined by prevailing social, economic, cultural, climatic, ecological and other conditions, while "sustainability" incorporates the notion of long-term availability and accessibility.

8. The Committee considers that the core content of the right to adequate food implies:

The availability of food in a quantity and quality sufficient to satisfy the dietary needs of individuals, free from adverse substances, and acceptable within a given culture;

The accessibility of such food in ways that are sustainable and that do not interfere with the enjoyment of other human rights.

9. *Dietary needs* implies that the diet as a whole contains a mix of nutrients for physical and mental growth, development and maintenance, and physical activity that are in compliance with human physiological needs at all stages throughout the life cycle and according to gender and occupation. Measures may therefore need to be taken to maintain, adapt or strengthen dietary diversity and appropriate consumption and feeding patterns, including breast-feeding, while ensuring that changes in availability and access to food supply as a minimum do not negatively affect dietary composition and intake.

10. *Free from adverse substances* sets requirements for food safety and for a range of protective measures by both public and private means to prevent contamination of foodstuffs through adulteration and/or through bad environmental hygiene or inappropriate handling at different stages throughout the food chain; care must also be taken to identify and avoid or destroy naturally occurring toxins.

11. *Cultural or consumer acceptability* implies the need also to take into account, as far as possible, perceived non nutrient-based values attached to food and food consumption and informed consumer concerns regarding the nature of accessible food supplies.

12. *Availability* refers to the possibilities either for feeding oneself directly from productive land or other natural resources, or for well functioning distribution, processing and market systems that can move food from the site of production to where it is needed in accordance with demand.

13. *Accessibility* encompasses both economic and physical accessibility:

Economic accessibility implies that personal or household financial costs associated with the acquisition of food for an adequate diet should be at a level such that the attainment and satisfaction of other basic needs are not threatened or compromised. Economic accessibility applies to any acquisition pattern or entitlement through which people procure their food and is a measure of the extent to which it is satisfactory for the enjoyment of the right to adequate food. Socially vulnerable groups such as landless persons and other particularly impoverished segments of the population may need attention through special programmes.

Physical accessibility implies that adequate food must be accessible to everyone, including physically vulnerable individuals, such as infants and young children, elderly people, the physically disabled, the terminally ill and persons with persistent medical problems, including the mentally ill. Victims of natural disasters, people living in disaster-prone areas and other specially disadvantaged groups may need special attention and sometimes priority consideration with respect to accessibility of food. A particular vulnerability is that of many indigenous population groups whose access to their ancestral lands may be threatened.

Obligations and violations

14. The nature of the legal obligations of States parties are set out in article 2 of the Covenant and has been dealt with in the Committee's General Comment No. 3 (1990). The principal obligation is to take steps to achieve *progressively* the full realization of the right to adequate food. This imposes an obligation to move as expeditiously as possible towards that goal. Every State is obliged to ensure for everyone under its jurisdiction access to the minimum essential food which is sufficient, nutritionally adequate and safe, to ensure their freedom from hunger.

15. The right to adequate food, like any other human right, imposes three types or levels of obligations on States parties: the obligations to *respect*, to *protect* and to *fulfil*. In turn, the obligation to *fulfil* incorporates both an obligation to *facilitate* and an obligation to *provide*.[1/] The obligation to *respect* existing access to adequate food requires States parties not to take any measures that result in preventing such access. The obligation to *protect* requires measures by the State to ensure that enterprises or individuals do not deprive individuals of their access to adequate food. The obligation to *fulfil (facilitate)* means the State must pro-actively engage in activities intended to strengthen people's access to and utilization of resources and means to ensure their livelihood, including food security. Finally, whenever an individual or group is unable, for reasons beyond their control, to enjoy the right to adequate food by the means at their disposal, States have the obligation to *fulfil (provide)* that right directly. This obligation also applies for persons who are victims of natural or other disasters.

16. Some measures at these different levels of obligations of States parties are of a more immediate nature, while other measures are more of a long-term character, to achieve progressively the full realization of the right to food.

17. Violations of the Covenant occur when a State fails to ensure the satisfaction of, at the very least, the minimum essential level required to be free from hunger. In determining which actions or omissions amount to a violation of the right to food, it is important to distinguish the inability from the unwillingness of a State party to comply. Should a State party argue that resource constraints make it impossible to provide access to food for those who are unable by themselves to secure such access, the State has to demonstrate that every effort has been made to use all the resources at its disposal in an effort to satisfy, as a matter of priority, those minimum obligations. This follows from Article 2.1 of the Covenant, which obliges a State party to take the necessary steps to the maximum of its available resources, as previously pointed out by the Committee in its General Comment No. 3, paragraph 10. A State claiming that it is unable to carry out its obligation for reasons beyond its control therefore has the burden of proving that this is the case and that it has unsuccessfully sought to obtain international support to ensure the availability and accessibility of the necessary food.

18. Furthermore, any discrimination in access to food, as well as to means and entitlements for its procurement, on the grounds of race, colour, sex, language, age, religion, political or other opinion, national or social origin, property, birth or other status with the purpose or effect of nullifying or impairing the equal enjoyment or exercise of economic, social and cultural rights constitutes a violation of the Covenant.

19. Violations of the right to food can occur through the direct action of States or other entities insufficiently regulated by States. These include: the formal repeal or suspension of legislation necessary for the continued enjoyment of the right to food; denial of access to food to particular individuals or groups, whether the discrimination is based on legislation or is pro-active; the prevention of access to humanitarian food aid in internal conflicts or other emergency situations; adoption of legislation or policies which are manifestly incompatible with pre-existing legal obligations relating to the right to food; and failure to regulate activities of individuals or groups so as to prevent them from violating the right to food of others, or the failure of a State to take into account its international legal obligations regarding the right to food when entering into agreements with other States or with international organizations.

20. While only States are parties to the Covenant and are thus ultimately accountable for compliance with it, all members of society — individuals, families, local communities, non-governmental organizations, civil society organizations, as well as the private business sector — have responsibilities in the realization of the right to adequate food. The State should provide an environment that facilitates implementation of these responsibilities. The private business sector — national and transnational — should pursue its activities within the framework of a code of conduct conducive to respect of the right to adequate food, agreed upon jointly with the Government and civil society.

Implementation at the national level

21. The most appropriate ways and means of implementing the right to adequate food will inevitably vary significantly from one State party to another. Every State will have a margin of discretion in choosing its own approaches, but the Covenant clearly requires that each State party take whatever steps are necessary to ensure that everyone is free from hunger and as soon as possible can enjoy the right to adequate food. This will require the adoption of a national strategy to ensure food and nutrition security for all, based on human rights principles that define the objectives, and the formulation of policies and corresponding benchmarks. It should also identify the resources available to meet the objectives and the most cost-effective way of using them.

22. The strategy should be based on a systematic identification of policy measures and activities relevant to the situation and context, as derived from the normative content of the right to adequate food and spelled out in relation to the levels and nature of State parties' obligations referred to in paragraph 15 of the present general comment. This will facilitate coordination between ministries and regional and local authorities and ensure that related policies and administrative decisions are in compliance with the obligations under article 11 of the Covenant.

23. The formulation and implementation of national strategies for the right to food requires full compliance with the principles of accountability, transparency, people's participation, decentralization, legislative capacity and the independence of the judiciary. Good governance is essential to the realization of all human rights, including the elimination of poverty and ensuring a satisfactory livelihood for all.

24. Appropriate institutional mechanisms should be devised to secure a representative process towards the formulation of a strategy, drawing on all available domestic expertise relevant to food and nutrition. The strategy should set out the responsibilities and time-frame for the implementation of the necessary measures.

25. The strategy should address critical issues and measures in regard to all aspects of the food system, including the production, processing, distribution, marketing and consumption of safe food, as well as parallel measures in the fields of health, education, employment and social security. Care should be taken to ensure the most sustainable management and use of natural and other resources for food at the national, regional, local and household levels.

26. The strategy should give particular attention to the need to prevent discrimination in access to food or resources for food. This should include: guarantees of full and equal access to economic resources, particularly for women, including the right to inheritance and the ownership of land and other property, credit, natural resources and appropriate technology; measures to respect and protect self-employment and work which provides a remuneration ensuring a decent living for wage earners and their families (as stipulated in article 7 (a) (ii) of the Covenant); maintaining registries on rights in land (including forests).

27. As part of their obligations to protect people's resource base for food, States parties should take appropriate steps to ensure that activities of the private business sector and civil society are in conformity with the right to food.

28. Even where a State faces severe resource constraints, whether caused by a process of economic adjustment, economic recession, climatic conditions or other factors, measures should be undertaken to ensure that the right to adequate food is especially fulfilled for vulnerable population groups and individuals.

Benchmarks and framework legislation
29. In implementing the country-specific strategies referred to above, States should set verifiable benchmarks for subsequent national and international monitoring. In this connection, States should consider the adoption of a *framework law* as a major instrument in the implementation of the national strategy concerning the right to food. The framework law should include provisions on its purpose; the targets or goals to be achieved and the time-frame to be set for the achievement of those targets; the means by which the purpose could be achieved described in broad terms, in particular the intended collaboration with civil society and the private sector and with international organizations; institutional responsibility for the process; and the national mechanisms for its monitoring, as well as possible recourse procedures. In developing the benchmarks and framework legislation, States parties should actively involve civil society organizations.

30. Appropriate United Nations programmes and agencies should assist, upon request, in drafting the framework legislation and in reviewing the sectoral legislation. FAO, for example, has considerable expertise and accumulated knowledge concerning legislation in the field of food and agriculture. The United Nations Children's Fund (UNICEF) has equivalent expertise concerning legislation with regard to the right to adequate food for infants and young children through maternal and child protection including legislation to enable breast-feeding, and with regard to the regulation of marketing of breast milk substitutes.

Monitoring
31. States parties shall develop and maintain mechanisms to monitor progress towards the realization of the right to adequate food for all, to identify the factors and difficulties affecting the degree of implementation of their obligations, and to facilitate the adoption of corrective legislation and administrative measures, including measures to implement their obligations under articles 2.1 and 23 of the Covenant.

Remedies and accountability
32. Any person or group who is a victim of a violation of the right to adequate food should have access to effective judicial or other appropriate remedies at both national and international levels. All victims of such violations are entitled to adequate reparation, which may take the form of restitution, compensation, satisfaction or guarantees of non-repetition. National Ombudsmen and human rights commissions should address violations of the right to food.

33. The incorporation in the domestic legal order of international instruments recognizing the right to food, or recognition of their applicability, can significantly enhance the scope and effectiveness of remedial measures and should be encouraged in all cases. Courts would then be empowered to adjudicate violations of the core content of the right to food by direct reference to obligations under the Covenant.

34. Judges and other members of the legal profession are invited to pay greater attention to violations of the right to food in the exercise of their functions.

35. States parties should respect and protect the work of human rights advocates and other members of civil society who assist vulnerable groups in the realization of their right to adequate food.

International obligations

States parties

36. In the spirit of article 56 of the Charter of the United Nations, the specific provisions contained in articles 11, 2.1, and 23 of the Covenant and the Rome Declaration of the World Food Summit, States parties should recognize the essential role of international cooperation and comply with their commitment to take joint and separate action to achieve the full realization of the right to adequate food. In implementing this commitment, States parties should take steps to respect the enjoyment of the right to food in other countries, to protect that right, to facilitate access to food and to provide the necessary aid when required. States parties should, in international agreements whenever relevant, ensure that the right to adequate food is given due attention and consider the development of further international legal instruments to that end.

37. States parties should refrain at all times from food embargoes or similar measures which endanger conditions for food production and access to food in other countries. Food should never be used as an instrument of political and economic pressure. In this regard, the Committee recalls its position, stated in its General Comment No. 8, on the relationship between economic sanctions and respect for economic, social and cultural rights.

States and international organizations

38. States have a joint and individual responsibility, in accordance with the Charter of the United Nations, to cooperate in providing disaster relief and humanitarian assistance in times of emergency, including assistance to refugees and internally displaced persons. Each State should contribute to this task in accordance with its ability. The role of the World Food Programme (WFP) and the Office of the United Nations High Commissioner for Refugees (UNHCR), and increasingly that of UNICEF and FAO is of particular importance in this respect and should be strengthened. Priority in food aid should be given to the most vulnerable populations.

39. Food aid should, as far as possible, be provided in ways which do not adversely affect local producers and local markets, and should be organized in ways that facilitate the return to food self-reliance of the beneficiaries. Such aid should be based on the needs of the intended beneficiaries. Products included in international food trade or aid programmes must be safe and culturally acceptable to the recipient population.

The United Nations and other international organizations

40. The role of the United Nations agencies, including through the United Nations Development Assistance Framework (UNDAF) at the country level, in promoting the realization of the right to food is of special importance. Coordinated efforts for the realization of the right to food should be maintained to enhance coherence and interaction among all the actors concerned, including the various components of civil society. The food organizations, FAO, WFP and the International Fund for Agricultural Development (IFAD) in conjunction with the United Nations Development Programme (UNDP), UNICEF, the World Bank and the regional development banks, should cooperate more effectively, building on their respective expertise, on the implementation of the right to food at the national level, with due respect to their individual mandates.

41. The international financial institutions, notably the International Monetary Fund (IMF) and the World Bank, should pay greater attention to the protection of the right to food in their lending policies and credit agreements and in international measures to deal with the debt crisis. Care should be taken, in line with the Committee's General Comment No. 2, paragraph 9, in any structural adjustment programme to ensure that the right to food is protected.